THE RADICAL POLITICS OF
THOMAS JEFFERSON

The horizon of history is still open. If the remembrance of things past would become a motive power in the struggle for changing the world, the struggle would be waged for a revolution hitherto suppressed in the previous historical revolutions.

—Herbert Marcuse

THE RADICAL POLITICS OF
THOMAS JEFFERSON

A Revisionist View

RICHARD K. MATTHEWS

UNIVERSITY PRESS OF KANSAS

For my family,
who always support but never understand;
and Deborah Jean,
who always understands but rarely agrees.

Published by the University Press of Kansas (Lawrence,
Kansas 66049), which was organized by the
Kansas Board of Regents and is operated and funded by
Emporia State University, Fort Hays State University,
Kansas State University, Pittsburg State University, the
University of Kansas, and Wichita State University

Library of Congress Cataloging in Publication Data
Matthews, Richard K., 1952–
The radical politics of Thomas Jefferson.
Bibliography: p.
Includes index.
1. Jefferson, Thomas,
1743–1826—Political and social
views.   2. Political science—United States—History—
18th century.   3. Political science—United States—
History—19th century.   I. Title.
E332.2.M37   1984   973.4'6'0924   84-5240
ISBN 0-7006-0256-9
ISBN 0-7006-0293-3 (pbk.)

Printed in the United States of America
10 9 8 7

Contents

Preface
to the Paperback Edition

This is a work of political *theory*. As such, it is inherently interpretive as well as normative.

The quotation by Jefferson that opens the first chapter of the book and creates the thematic tone for the presentation that follows emphatically makes a point about the interpretive enterprise: "The moment a person forms a theory his imagination sees in every object only the traits which favor that theory." Jefferson's acute observation applies to all theories, all interpretive efforts, including this book. It may well be that there is no single, authoritative portrait of Thomas Jefferson, only variations on a theme.

As with all efforts in constructing theory, this book attempts to present Jefferson's political theory as parsimoniously and elegantly as possible. While both parsimony and elegance are desirable in the creation of interpretive theory, discrimination and explanation are also essential. The interpretation must be able to separate itself from other theoretical approaches while striving to explain more fully the material under investigation. In the present context, the material consists of the enormous mass of Jefferson's known writings, which exist in the form of thousands of letters, dozens of speeches, treatises, and tracts, and a single book. Because Jefferson never systematically detailed his political theory, this book attempts to do so. It strives to construct his political theory concisely, to explain how his political ideas compose a theoretical whole, and to separate itself from prior interpretive efforts.

The opening quotation also highlights another salient feature of political theory—that is, the presence of imagination. Political theory concerns *vision*, particularly aesthetic vision. What vision of the beautiful, of the political, of humanity, does a political thinker hold? What imaginative vision of the future does the theory present? These are among the most basic and important questions confronting political theory. And they are obviously and enormously normative. It is specifically this imaginative dimension to Jefferson's politics, his vision, that becomes a primary focus of this book. The book is not, consequently, another study of either Jefferson the president, the governor, or the secretary of state; it is, rather, a critical evaluation and presentation of Jefferson the intellectual, the political theorist, the "idealist" dreamer. For ultimately it is precisely this Jefferson, Jefferson the dreamer, who can help rekindle the political dialogue over how and where the American polity should travel. Remember, it is not the feasibility but the meaning of Jefferson's vision that remains of political import: it contains the historic, if currently slumbering, tension between *what is* and *what ought to be*.

Finally, this book attempts to complement the recent work of those social and political historians who, in their critical reexamination of the formative years of the Republic, are demonstrating that American liberalism possesses its own unique, time-bound history. American liberalism, as a set of values, beliefs, and practices, has specific origins in time and space and has a subsequent history. Jefferson's radical politics stands in contrast to this liberal moment.

Except for correcting a few minor errors, this paperback edition is unchanged from the earlier, clothbound text. I would like, *in memoriam*, to acknowledge the unwavering support and boundless encouragement of my brother Paul

PREFACE

A. Pfretzschner. He gracefully touched my life, for which I will be forever grateful.

Richard K. Matthews
Department of Government
Lehigh University
Bethlehem, Pennsylvania

Acknowledgments

Many hands are involved in the process of writing, typing, editing, and rewriting a work of this length. Although the final responsibility rests with the author, it is appropriate to gratefully acknowledge the other participants in the process.

I want to thank Susan Smith, Ruth Panovec, and Marlene Bartholomew for their unending patience and skill as typists. Professors Charles Bednar, David Ingersoll, Howard Marblestone, Paul Pfretzschner, and Daniel Wilson read and commented on parts of the manuscript. The efforts of each of them improved the work, making it less imperfect than it would have been otherwise. My thanks, for things that cannot be expressed in an acknowledgment, to Jeffrey Burtaine, Paula Consolini, Stephen Lammers, James Lennertz, George Panichas, Asher Horowitz, Greg White, Andy Davison, and Andy Zlotnick. I also gratefully acknowledge the presence of Zachary Daniel, who already has taught me more about life than I ever dreamed possible.

1

The "Jeffersonian" Tradition: The Future of an Illusion

The moment a person forms a theory his imagination sees in every object only the traits which favor that theory.[1]

—Jefferson

Works on Thomas Jefferson abound. Scores of books, hundreds of articles, and reams of paper have been published on virtually every facet of his life. It is doubtful that any other American political thinker has received as intensive or extensive a scrutiny as he has.[2] And yet it is equally questionable if any other founding father has been more seriously misrepresented, as well as misunderstood.[3]

During the past quarter of a century, in anticipation of the bicentennial celebration of the founding of the United States, the subject of the American Revolution has come under increasing scholarly investigation. The history of the history of the revolution and of the intellectual debate surrounding it is in itself important and worthy of discussion. Written in the early nineteen hundreds, J. Allen Smith's *The Spirit of the American Government* laid the primary groundwork and drew the thematic lines for what future historians would eventually call the conflict interpretation of American history.[4] Smith viewed the history of the United States as a continuing struggle between the forces of democracy, embodied in the Declaration of Independence, and those of aristocracy, expressed in the Constitution. With the issue framed by Smith, it was possible for Charles Beard to give the theory its most famous, if not always its most logical, airing.

Directly inspired by the writings of Frederick Jackson Turner, Beard's *An Economic Interpretation of the Constitution of the United States* was misread from the start.[5] Some of the confusion surrounding the book undoubtedly resulted from

1

its ambiguous title. Only one chapter, and that an exceptionally brief one, even attempts to offer any interpretation, economic or other, of the Constitution per se. Rather, Beard examines the socioeconomic background of the delegates to the Constitutional Convention in the hope of deducing their ulterior motives. After carefully explaining that he is offering but one possible interpretation of this event—an interpretation that he insists is not based on economic determinism—Beard concludes from his analysis that a class division existed between the supporters and the opponents of the Constitution.[6] Its advocates were the men of "money, public securities, manufactures, and trade and shipping." To no one's surprise, Beard finds that "the Constitution was essentially an economic document based upon the concept that the fundamental private rights of property are anterior to government and morally beyond the reach of popular majorities."[7] Here, then, is Beard's statement of conflict in American history: the rights of property and the Constitution, versus the rights of man as articulated in the Declaration of Independence. Though the former have triumphed, the latter are always present and are likely to reappear, if only to divert, guide, or rechannel the driving dynamic of economics.[8]

The second major spokesperson for the conflict historians is Vernon L. Parrington, whose *Main Currents in American Thought* skyrocketed to fame and then, with equal abruptness, plummeted to oblivion.[9] An extended, though perhaps not penetrating, inspection of the literary aspect of American politics, Parrington's work reaches a Manichean interpretation of history that lies between liberal and antiliberal thought.[10] The line of liberalism, traced back through Roger Williams, Benjamin Franklin, and Thomas Jefferson, is juxtaposed to the line of John Cotton, Jonathan Edwards, and Alexander Hamilton, "men whose grandiose dreams envisaged different ends for America."[11] The liberals were the champions of "justice and the rights of man"; the antiliberals were the advocates of "exploitation and the rights of trade."[12] Like Beard, Parrington believed that these two

2

driving forces constituted the dynamic source of American history from its genesis to the present.[13]

Perhaps the most fruitful immediate by-product of the efforts by the progressive historians came from the reaction they generated during the period at the end of the Second World War, the beginning of the cold war, and Daniel Bell's seminal *End of Ideology*.[14] This school, known as the consensus approach, rejects the notion that American history is the result of conflict between diametrically opposed economic or philosophic forces; indeed, it finds a remarkable lack of conflict in American history. Moreover, whatever conflict exists is seen as a fraternal quarrel among men of similar political persuasions. History, then, becomes the virtually unconscious unfolding of a new nation which has been providentially extricated from the forces of real conflict that are found in the more complex European setting.[15] The notion of conflict is replaced with the idea of an all-pervasive American consensus on political values. As in the case of the conflict historians, two names stand out from the rest: Daniel Boorstin and Louis Hartz.

Both authors use Alexis de Tocqueville's classic *Democracy in America* as their starting point.[16] "Born equal," Americans did not have "to endure a democratic revolution." Since Americans neither needed nor developed a conscious political awareness, American history became but the inevitable response to the unique political situation of a colony that was removed from the dynamic, crosscutting socioeconomic and ideological forces of Europe. This American moment of ecstasy is born out of the freedom of a new society to grow and develop in an abundant, pristine setting that is relatively independent of the antagonistic forces of European politics.

The first of the consensus efforts is Boorstin's *The Genius of American Politics*.[17] Anxious to have the United States pursue an isolationist policy in international relations, Boorstin argues: "No nation has ever believed more firmly that its political life was based on a perfect theory. And yet no nation has ever been less interested in political philosophy or produced less in the way of political theory."[18] It would be "un-American" to encourage other countries "to adopt our 'philosophy' because America has no philosophy which can be exported."[19] The uniqueness of the American experience—what Boorstin calls its "genius"—makes it impossible for any other nation to emulate it: the "seamlessness," the homogeneity, of America made it a special case in world history.[20] Unabashedly, he pushes this point to its inevitable conclusion: "We have taken for granted that God himself drew the plans of our career and marked its outlines in our history and on our very ground."[21] Given its divine particularity, Boorstin asks, "Does the United States need political philosophy?" Rhetorically he answers: "We thus find engraved in our national consciousness the belief that values somehow emerged from the American experience; that we do not need American philosophers because we already have an American philosophy, implicit in the American Way of Life."[22] In more erudite tones, Louis Hartz's *The Liberal Tradition in America* helped to add substance and respect to Boorstin's impassioned efforts. More importantly, this brilliant work restructured the intellectual debate on the founding era.

Beginning with the same theme as Boorstin's—the uniqueness of the American experience—Hartz's theory attempts to make more than a mere explanation of the past. At the risk of being reductionistic, we may identify his intriguing and illuminating theory as follows. Detached from Europe and placed in the context of a virgin environment, the United States (and all new societies) lose the stimulus for change, which the whole of Europe provides.[23] More specifically, this amounts to a dual-factor theory of social dynamics: "the absence of feudalism and the presence of the liberal idea."[24] Unknowingly, America lives out the liberal dream of seventeenth-century England, but in isolation from both the material and the ideological countervailing forces of Europe, which profoundly shaped that dream in the mother country. In the new setting, the economic forces themselves become absorbed into the liberal ideology: both the farmer and the worker become parts of the framework of democratic liberalism.[25] In a new world, which is devoid of the full spectrum of political ideologies that are found in Europe, "the search for 'democratic theory,' or even 'political theory,' is a beguiling quest."[26] Having escaped the influences of feudalism, America lacks the revolutionary tradition which is linked both with the Puritan and French revolutions; what is more, it lacks also a tradition of reaction.[27] Hartz logically concludes that the American response to capitalism is really not an anticapitalist response at all. Although John Taylor's agrarian theory had a "Marxian touch," it was really a quest on behalf of the capitalist farmer against other interests.[28] Legitimate socialist as well as reactionary responses, quite simply, were outside the universe of American political discourse: America was captive of the bourgeois frame of reference of that quintessential English liberal John Locke. As Hartz summarized his thesis, "Locke dominates American political thought, as no thinker anywhere dominates the political thought of a nation."[29]

Locke's hegemonic reign was short-lived. The debate among scholars gained fuel from a group of "Neo-Whig" historians, led by Bernard Bailyn, Gordon Wood, and J. G. A. Pocock.[30] Bailyn's analysis established what one historian has called "a new paradigm for interpreting the Revolution."[31] The new paradigm is actually an old paradigm, which was originally drawn from English politics during the age of the Dissenters, the radical Whigs, the Classical Republicans, the Commonwealthmen, members of the Country party, or, more simply, all of the groups that constituted the Opposition to Sir Robert Walpole.[32] English Republican theory, then, attempts to replace Lockean liberalism as the key to decoding and comprehending the American Revolution. Bailyn further argued that "the outbreak of the Revolution was not the result of social discontent, or of economic disturbances, or of rising misery." Instead, it "was a response to acts of power deemed arbitrary, degrading, and uncontrollable—a response, in itself objectively reasonable, that was inflamed to the point of explosion by ideological currents generating fears everywhere in America that irresponsible and self-seeking adventurers—what the twentieth century would call political gangsters—had gained the power of the English government and were turning first, for reasons that were variously explained, to that Rhineland of their aggressions, the colonies."[33] Here the Republican language of virtue and corruption, liberty and oppression, is manifest. Continuing the attack on the Progressive historians and the conflict school, Bailyn alters Hartz's approach to consensus by replacing Lockean liberalism with English republicanism.

The republican paradigmatic approach is extended beyond the revolutionary years through the Constitution and the Federalist-Republican debate in Gordon Wood's *The Creation of the American Republic*. Wood argues that the Constitution represents an "end of classical politics" and a beginning of a movement from republicanism to liberalism: "The Constitution represented both the climax and the finale of the American Enlightenment, both the fulfillment and the end of the belief that the endless variety and perplexity of society could be reduced to a simple and harmonious system. By attempting to formulate a theory of politics that would represent reality as it was, the Americans of 1787 shattered the classical Whig world of 1776." This new, postclassical world view required an altered perspective of the people. "Once the people were thought to be composed of various interests in opposition to one another, all sense of a graduated organic chain in the social hierarchy became irrelevant. . . . The people were not an order organically tied together by their unity of interest but rather an agglomeration of hostile individuals coming together for their mutual benefit to construct a society."[34] Wood, then, sees the Constitution as the beginning emergence of modern liberal politics.

The latest and most impressive of the Neo-Whig efforts is J. G. A. Pocock's enormously influential *The Machiavellian Moment: Florentine Political Thought and the Atlantic Republican Tradition*. Once again emphasizing the necessity of replacing Lockean liberalism with republicanism, Pocock traces the fountainhead of this paradigm back to its origins in Florentine thought—during the era of Machiavelli, the resuscitation of civic humanism, and the flowering of Aristotelianism. As Pocock explains it, "In this book we have been concerned with another tradition, reducible to the sequence of Aristotle's thesis that human nature is civic and Machiavelli's thesis that, in the world of secular time where alone the polis can exist, this nature of man may never be more than partially and contradictorily realized. Virtue can develop only in time, but is always threatened with corruption by time." To Pocock, "the Machiavellian moment" is more than just the time frame in which Machiavellian thought made its appearance; rather, it also represents an ongoing problem in political theory. "It is asserted that certain enduring patterns in the temporal consciousness of medieval and early modern Europeans led to the presentation of the republic, and the citizen's participation in it, as constituting a problem in historical self-understanding." Making further clarification, he adds that

> "the Machiavellian moment" denotes the problem itself. It is a name for the moment in conceptualized time in which the republic was seen as confronting its own temporal finitude, as attempting to remain morally and politically stable in a stream of irrational events conceived as essentially destructive of all systems of secular stability. In the language which had been developed for the purpose, this was spoken of as the confrontation of "virtue" with "fortune" and "corruption."

Creating "an important paradigmatic legacy" with concepts of balanced government, *virtu*, commerce, corruption, empire and the role of arms and property, this moment is transplanted to England and America, where, if Pocock is correct, it exercised the hegemony that Hartz claimed for John Locke. Consequently, while Gordon Wood argues that the Constitution of 1787 represents a shift away from republicanism toward liberalism, Pocock sees it as a continuation of the civic-humanist tradition. Through Pocock's republican reading, the creation of the American republic becomes an attempted "flight from history"; born "in dread of modern-

7

ity," the United States tries to escape the ravages of history by means of civic virtue.[35]

This ideological school, which emphasizes civic humanism rather than liberal individualism, has generated its own critical response. There are those critics, some centering around Merrill Jensen, who have revived the concern of the early conflict historians by documenting the acute social tensions and the clashing interests in colonial America.[36] And there are other scholars who question the legitimacy of the republican rereading itself, essentially arguing that liberalism is still the important intellectual foundation to understanding the American Revolution. Isaac Kramnick cryptically captures the essence of the criticism: "To paraphrase Mark Twain, the scholarly consensus on Locke's death in the late eighteenth century is greatly exaggerated."[37] The historiographic debate among the various perspectives over the founding era has proved, at times, rather vociferous; and the question of which hegemonic paradigm—Lockean liberalism or civic humanism—is to be employed to interpret the thought of the era has had an impact on studies focusing specifically on Jefferson.[38]

Even before Hartz established the dominance of Locke, most studies saw Jefferson as an American extension of Lockean liberalism. Carl Becker's classic *The Declaration of Independence* (1922) established a Locke-Jefferson connection that remained relatively unchallenged until recently. After explaining that there may appear to be a certain logic to thinking that Jefferson may have been influenced by French political thought, since questions of independence were being hotly debated on the Continent, Becker dismisses the notion, claiming that "it does not appear that Jefferson, or any other American, read many French books." Becker therefore concludes: "So far as the 'Fathers' were, before 1776, directly influenced by particular writers, the writers were English, and notably Locke"; and regarding Jefferson in particular, "the lineage is direct: Jefferson copied Locke."[39]

Many authors have challenged Becker's thesis, but in 1978

two books, *Inventing America: Jefferson's Declaration of Independence*, by Garry Wills, and *The Philosophy of the American Revolution*, by Morton White, persuasively argued that the roots of Jefferson's political ideas are to be located in the Scottish Enlightenment. Now, this is an old connection, which had been argued as early as 1907 by I. Woodbridge Riley in *American Philosophy*, then in greater detail by Adrienne Koch in *The Philosophy of Thomas Jefferson* (1943). But what Wills in particular accomplished was to give the question of Locke versus the Scots wide public attention.[40] This notoriety made Wills's portrait the object of several scathing critiques. The most insightful of these reviews is by Judith Shklar, who, while acknowledging the book's shortcomings, still captures the importance of Wills's work: "The outcome is terrible intellectual history, but oddly a convincing picture of Jefferson does emerge."[41] While both Wills and White agree on the importance of the Scottish Enlightenment, they disagree on which particular thinkers and which particular thoughts are germane. For Wills, the sentimentalist philosophy of Francis Hutcheson is the Jeffersonian taproot; for White, it is the rationalism of Thomas Reid, Henry Home (Lord Kames), and Richard Price. In spite of their differences over points of genesis, both Wills and White find in Jefferson a communitarian, or organic, conception of man, as opposed to the liberal individualism most often associated with his name.

While not denying a Scottish flavor to much of Jefferson, other scholars locate the influential source of his ideas neither in Locke nor in the Scots. Gilbert Chinard, in *The Letters of Lafayette and Jefferson* (1929), Adrienne Koch, in both *The Philosophy of Thomas Jefferson* (1943) and *Jefferson and Madison: The Great Collaboration* (1950), and Daniel Boorstin, in *The Lost World of Thomas Jefferson* (1948), emphasize, à la Vernon Parrington, the importance of French thought to understanding Jefferson. In spite of Paul Spurlin's *Rousseau in America: 1760–1809* (1969), in which he concludes that "it is obvious that Rousseau had vogue but not influence in eighteenth-century America," it is ironic that J. G. A.

9

Pocock's work may yet breathe life back into the French influence.[42] At several points in *The Machiavellian Moment*, Pocock enigmatically suggests that America, in Jefferson, may have experienced more of a "Rousseauean moment" than a Machiavellian one.[43]

The country-court debate within the republican paradigm has generated many new pieces on Jefferson and the other founders. Among the most important of these are Lance Banning's *The Jeffersonian Persuasion* (1978), Forrest McDonald's *The Presidency of Thomas Jefferson* (1976), Gerald Stourzh's *Alexander Hamilton and the Idea of Republican Government* (1970), Garry Wills's *Explaining America* (1981), and Drew McCoy's *The Elusive Republic: Political Economy in Jeffersonian America* (1980). Even though Banning was among the first to carefully detail the connection between the new Republican party and the old Country party, it is McDonald who sets out to demonstrate Professor Thomas D. Govan's questionable statement that "just about everything in Jeffersonian Republicanism was to be found in Bolingbroke" and, like McCoy, concludes that Jefferson, in dread of modernity, desired a return to "some Edenic Past."[44] While Stourzh clearly demonstrates the importance of Hume, Hobbes, and Blackstone to understanding Hamilton as a "modern" rather than as an "old" Whig, it is Wills who shows the similarity, and yet subtle differences, between Hamilton and Madison at the time of *The Federalist Papers*. Still, it is McCoy's work that is particularly illustrative of one of the central difficulties in the Jefferson industry—namely, the unquestioned identification of Thomas Jefferson with an idea system called "Jeffersonian." This is an old problem. It can be found in Beard's *Economic Origins of Jeffersonian Democracy* and in Boorstin's vivid articulation of a world view associated with Jefferson and "the Jeffersonians" in *The Lost World of Thomas Jefferson*, as well as Banning's *The Jeffersonian Persuasion*. McCoy explains his title, *The Elusive Republic: Political Economy in Jeffersonian America*, thus:

> By "Jeffersonian" I refer to a specific configuration of assumptions, fears, beliefs, and values that shaped a vision of

expansion across space—the American continent—as a necessary alternative to the development through time that was generally thought to bring with it both political corruption and social decay. My analysis suggests that this Jeffersonian vision reflected the dominant ideological strain of republican political economy in Revolutionary and early national America. As a cast of mind, it will be explored in this study largely, but not exclusively, through a close consideration of such leading thinkers and policymakers as Benjamin Franklin, Thomas Jefferson, and especially James Madison.[45]

McCoy's reliance on "especially Madison" is exactly the point. Citing Madison far more often than he cites Jefferson, McCoy should have titled his work "Madisonian America," for it is Madison, not Jefferson, who is being described. This raises the curious question of whether or not Jefferson is really a Jeffersonian at all. When "Jeffersonian" really means "Madisonian," as in McCoy's study, the answer is certainly not: Madison embraces a fatalistic view of the future which makes him reluctant to engage the inevitable demise of the republic, while Jefferson possesses an unwavering faith in humanity's ability to make its own history.

Not unlike McCoy, Pocock also uses the terms *Jefferson* and *Jeffersonian* interchangeably. Beginning with the premise that Jefferson was part of a republican tradition in America that seeks quixotically "a flight from modernity and a future no less than from antiquity and a past," Pocock reads this tradition back into Jefferson; he also finds a Jefferson who is afraid of a future when "the reservoir of land must be exhausted and the expansion of virtue will no longer keep ahead of the progress of commerce." Pocock then draws a Madisonian conclusion but attributes it to Jefferson: "When that point is reached, the process of corruption must be resumed; men will become dependent upon each other in a market economy and dependent on government in great cities."[46] For Jefferson, this alienating condition will happen only if democratic man does not keep his laws in pace with the changes of circumstances—probably the central concern in all of Jefferson's political theory. So long as men keep their lives and laws in harmony, then the future—at least for

Jefferson—is to be embraced. It is Madison, then, who sees corruption and collapse as inevitable; and if anyone is to be linked to the "politics of nostalgia," it is he rather than Jefferson.

In addition to the civic-humanist historians, the earlier, liberal reading of Jefferson still has its advocates. The most impressive of the recent efforts along this more-traditional line of interpretation can be found in the important work of Joyce Appleby. Noting Jefferson's optimism and hopes for the future, Appleby finds questionable at least two aspects to the republican interpretation of Jefferson.[47] "The civic-humanist tradition also fostered suspicions about commercial development and economic innovation, which both Jefferson and his *Americanist* friends strongly favored." And concerning the civic-humanist view of where individuals were to find fulfillment, in the public or in the private realm, she asserts that Jefferson "reversed the priorities implicit in the classical tradition. The private came first. Instead of regarding the public arena as the locus of human fulfillment where men rose above their self-interest . . . , Jefferson wanted government to offer protection to the personal realm where men might freely exercise their faculties."[48]

Appleby's criticism of the republican reading of Jefferson is, for the most part, accurate: Jefferson looks forward to the future. However, in attempting to turn Jefferson into an advocate of early liberal capitalism, Appleby appears to be on weaker ground. For while Jefferson did indeed want government protection for individual development, his individual was closer to, though not identical with, *homo civicus* than *homo oeconomicus*.[49] Jefferson's position on the good life is more Aristotelean than most of the liberal theorists have admitted. Indeed, like Aristotle, who was the first to articulate the uniqueness of man as *zoon politikon*, Jefferson also believes that the *vita contemplativa*, nevertheless, is the highest activity.

Appleby also finds objectionable the "agrarian myth" interpretation of Jefferson inspired by Richard Hofstadter's *The Age of Reform*.[50] In the agrarian myth, Jefferson is drawn to the noncommercial, nonpecuniary, self-sufficient dimensions of farming. "The agrarian myth makes him a traditional, republican visionary, social radical perhaps, but economically conservative." Fully aware of the impact that historiography has upon understanding the past, Appleby persuasively argues that "the instantaneous popularity of Hofstadter's 'agrarian myth' owes a good deal more to trends in the writing of history than to the evidentiary base upon which it rested." Whether it is the agrarian myth or the civic-humanist interpretation, Appleby finds both views problematic: Jefferson is "not the heroic loser in a battle against modernity, but the conspicuous winner in a contest over how the government should serve its citizens in the first generation of the nation's territorial expansion."[51] Appleby's Jefferson, then, is "both democratic and capitalistic, agrarian and commercial." Rather than viewing agriculture "as a venerable form of production giving shelter to a traditional way of life," Jefferson believes that "progressive agricultural development" can assist "ordinary men" in escaping "the tyranny of their social superiors both as employers and magistrates."[52] Where other twentieth-century historians read back into Jefferson an anticommercial bias, Appleby locates "a commitment to growth through the unimpeded exertions of individuals whose access to economic opportunity was both protected and facilitated by government."[53] In contrast to his being an opponent of commercial development, Appleby believes that Jefferson is an advocate of a fascinating new form of economic organization called capitalism.

> In the eighteenth century two features of the market economy fascinated contemporaries: the reliance upon individual initiative and the absence of authoritarian direction. Increasingly private arrangements were counted upon to supply the public's material needs. At the same time the productive goal of making wealth to produce wealth supplanted the older notion of wealth as the maintainer of status. In these transformations we come close to the conceptual heart of capitalism, for money becomes capital through the changed

intentions of those with the money, that is, with the decision to invest rather than spend or hoard wealth.[54]

Capital—its production and reproduction—is certainly the conceptual heart of capitalism. But it is not the heart of Jefferson. The very terms of this debate—namely procapitalist versus anticapitalist, or procommerce versus anticommerce—attempt to constrict Jefferson to a particular economic frame of reference which is too confining to his vision. Neither wealth nor capital ever constitutes the conceptual core of Jefferson. It is important, then, to move beyond the economic language of liberal capitalism if the real Jefferson is to emerge.

Even though the literature on the Revolutionary era has undergone several paradigmatic shifts and while the literature on Jefferson has reflected these changes, the Lockean liberal interpretation of Jefferson from Carl Becker to Joyce Appleby, among others, is still the common view. Rather than presenting an extended review of the literature on the liberal Jefferson, two descriptions from recent studies of American political theory can be taken as sufficiently illustrative of the liberal myth surrounding Jefferson.

In one text, *Ideology and Myth in American Politics* (1976), Mark Roelofs, the author, shares Louis Hartz's general view of American history; he finds little difference between Jefferson and Alexander Hamilton. The latter, he claims, "was an eighteenth century, English-style commercial liberal schooled in the works of Adam Smith and the rest, with a remarkable grasp of the practical needs of America's infant, capitalist economy." This description is accurate enough, but the author unfortunately goes on to claim that "Jefferson occupied much the same general ground philosophically, and the problem of distinguishing between his position and Hamilton's becomes one of shading and emphasis."[55] Max Skidmore's even-more-recent elaboration on American politics, *American Political Thought* (1978), neatly captures the "traditional Jefferson" with this brief introductory sentence: "Thomas Jefferson was fully within the liberal tradition."

After echoing the themes found in many other Jefferson studies, Skidmore diverts his readers' attention to an interesting anomaly in the normal Jeffersonian interpretation by exploring Hannah Arendt's analysis of Jefferson's writings on ward republics. At the end of his remarks on Arendt, he offers a prophetic comment, which is then quickly brushed aside: "If this [Arendt's Jefferson] is correct, . . . he must be regarded as vastly more radical than has been recognized."[56] That is, alas, precisely the point.

This widely held interpretation of Jefferson mistakenly views him as a traditional eighteenth-century liberal, perhaps even a liberal-democratic, theorist.[57] From that perspective, man is seen as an acquisitive, atomistic creature who prudentially enters civil society in order to protect his person and his property. Usually, man is believed to have natural rights to his person and property, which exist independent of and prior to the creation of government. His *telos* is the liberty to actively pursue ever-increasing amounts of power and/or property in order either to solidify or to advance his position in a mobile society composed of other like-minded acquirers. This perspective is the historic a priori schema which many scholars bring with them and read back into the writings of Jefferson. Given the absence of a magnum opus by Jefferson and given the presence of thousands of his public and private letters, all scholarly efforts to present an integrative understanding of his political ideas are forced to employ an eclectic method; hence it is understandable that a liberal(-democratic) myth surrounds his work: it is not only possible but also quite easy to find selective evidence to support such a perspective. Of course, the same tendency to read back into Jefferson whatever one wishes can be applied to the republican revisionists. As Jefferson explains, "The moment a person forms a theory his imagination sees in every object only the traits which favor that theory."

Nevertheless, four exceptions to the prevailing liberal mode of interpretation have recently been published. These important studies cast serious doubt on the continuing

15

validity of the traditional Jefferson and of the "Jeffersonian" tradition. Each of these anomalous interpretations deals with one component of Jefferson's ideas, rather than with his entire system. However, when each is removed from isolation and placed alongside the other three, a new interpretation of Jefferson is demanded.

Hannah Arendt's *On Revolution* was the first challenge to the tradition. By examining the function of ward-republics in Jefferson's politics, she shows the radical democratic nature behind his theory.[58] *The Machine in the Garden*, by Leo Marx, attacks the "agrarian" myth surrounding Jefferson by demonstrating that Jefferson's economic theory was based on a "pastoral ideal" that was distinctly noncapitalistic, rather than either anticapitalistic or petit-bourgeois.[59] Focusing on the traditional political-economic category of property, C. B. Macpherson, first in *Democratic Theory: Essays in Retrieval* and then in *The Life and Times of Liberal Democracy*, pushes Jefferson's arguments concerning property rights to their logical conclusions, which place Jefferson outside the economic system that is traditionally misassociated with his name.[60] Finally, the heart of the conventional Jefferson myth is fatally stabbed by Garry Wills in *Inventing America: Jefferson's Declaration of Independence*. Wills attacks the very core of the "liberal" Jefferson when he argues that Jefferson was not a Lockean liberal at all but, rather, "a Scottish-Enlightenment communitarian."[61]

When these four particular efforts at Jeffersonian exegesis are pieced into the patchwork quilt of Jefferson's political theory, a different, alternative Jefferson emerges: a Jefferson who not only presents a radical critique of American market society but also provides an image for—if not a road map to—a consciously made, legitimately democratic American future.

Specifically, this monograph will attempt to establish the following three themes concerning Jefferson's political philosophy and the scholarly tradition that clouds it.

First, Richard Hofstadter, Daniel Boorstin, and Louis Hartz, of the "end of ideology" era, are accurate in their observations that the contemporary United States does not have any legitimate philosophic alternative to its unique brand of market liberalism. But these scholars are, in a manner, incorrect in claiming that such an alternative never existed. Because Jefferson failed to write a magnum opus, he never left an obvious, systematic alternative to American liberalism. But by returning to his writings and by ordering the pieces of the Jeffersonian political puzzle, such a theoretical alternative can be constructed.

Second, even though Jefferson and Madison are often linked together by historians and political scientists in terms of their "great collaboration" of constructing a "Jeffersonian" America, they are, with regard to their political theories, qualitatively different. James Madison was both more market-oriented and more antidemocratic than is generally realized; ideologically, he stood closer to Alexander Hamilton than to Thomas Jefferson. However, by becoming linked with the Madison-Hamilton tradition, Jefferson, unwittingly or not, provides the ideological cover, the mythically democratic legitimatizing drapery, for the American market system that has existed from 1787 to the present.

Third, philosophically, Jefferson is beyond the early liberal-"democratic" tradition of the nineteenth century. Within the confines of that tradition he is to the left of John Stuart Mill, closer to T. H. Green or Jean-Jacques Rousseau. Jefferson's political philosophy possesses characteristics that are usually associated with three analytically separable traditions. (a) Humanism: his vehement arguments against economic exploitation and in favor of substantive economic and political freedom, while they are antimarket, are not, as J. G. A. Pocock and others believe, antimodern. The language of the civic-humanist paradigm is indeed helpful for understanding Jefferson; but his ideal human would balance the public and the private, for a life totally devoted to either would be less than fully human. (b) Communitarian anarchism: his study of the American Indians, which resulted in a deep admiration of these tribal communities, helped to convince Jefferson that man was a social, harmonious, cooperative, and just creature who, under the appropriate socioeconomic conditions, could happily live in a community that did not need the presence of the Leviathan. (c) Radical democracy: Jefferson argued the necessity for every generation to exercise its natural right to create anew its political life; this notion is intimately tied to his case for the automatic termination of all positive laws, including constitutions. Both of these positions are original Jeffersonian ideas which place him on the radical fringe of democratic theory. As Sheldon Wolin persuasively argues, "The roots of the divergence between the liberal and the radical democratic traditions lie in their contrasting faiths concerning the ability of the human mind to fathom reality and to translate the results into practical action."[62] Jefferson's faith in humanity's ability to govern itself is what separates him from someone like Rousseau and enables him sanguinely to leave all political problems to the succeeding generations.

At mid passage in the bicentennial anniversaries of the Declaration of Independence and the Constitution of the United States, an ongoing national celebration that is symptomatic of America's increasing tendency toward narcissism, it seems particularly appropriate to return to this founding era in an attempt to brush away some of the cobwebs of the past. Given Jefferson's unique role in the era, it is hoped that his own political ideas may provide a springboard for American political thought to move beyond the market liberalism of Madison and Hamilton cum Roosevelt to Reagan. For this to occur, it is first necessary to extricate Jefferson's theory from the myths that surround, envelop, and ultimately distort it.

2
Property: "The Earth Belongs to the Living"

I set out on this ground, which I suppose to be self-evident, "that the earth belongs in usufruct to the living": that the dead have neither powers nor rights over it.[1]

—Jefferson

Toward the final days of his tenure as United States minister to France, in the fateful year 1789, Jefferson sent to James Madison one of the more illuminating of his countless epistles. Caught up, no doubt, in the excitement of the impending revolution, he elected to take the opportunity to speculate openly on the nature of obligations between generations of men. Specifically, can one generation of society bind, either legally or morally, the succeeding one? Although property considerations form the central concern of the letter, the explicit political implications that are drawn and the questions that are raised by Jefferson place him outside the traditional Lockean-cum-Madisonian context of Anglo-American political theory, as the following analysis will demonstrate.

Even a brief, casual reading of this particular correspondence between Jefferson and Madison shows that he considered his inquiry *sui generis* and important.

> The question Whether one generation of men has a right to bind another, seems never to have been started either on this or our side of the water. Yet it is a question of such consequences as not only to merit decision, but place also, among the fundamental principles of every government.[2]

Before proceeding to present the rational grounds behind his response, Jefferson forewarns Madison by declaring his conclusion that "no such obligation can be so transmitted."

As is often the Jeffersonian style when writing theoretical papers, he constructs his argument upon first principles, the truth of which he claims is "self-evident." Appeals to intuition, or self-evidence, have a certain aristocratic flavor to them, especially when it is argued that only certain types of men, usually white male property holders, have the ability to discern these truths rationally.[3] However, Jefferson was a democrat. He believed that all men—regardless either of socioeconomic or of racial background—were capable of recognizing such truths. The reason is that Jefferson's argument does not rest on man's ability to reason; rather, it assumes that all men have a "moral sense." This discussion of the moral sense will be extended in the chapter on man. Here let it suffice to say that if men will but follow their moral sense, they can live in tranquility.

In this letter to Madison, there are at least two such self-evident truths: first, " 'that the earth belongs in usufruct to the living,' " and second, "that the dead have neither powers nor rights over it." Whenever a member of society dies, the control over the portion of land that he had a right to use while living reverts to society. Inheritance laws may be socially established. In the absence of such laws, appropriation goes to the first occupant, who, Jefferson assumes, will normally be a member of the deceased person's family.[4] Jefferson's point is that positive law, not natural right, creates property rights. "But the child, the legatee, or creditor takes it, not by any natural right, but by a law of the society of which they are members, and to which they are subject." Nor does any man, individually or collectively, have a natural right either to prescribe or to proscribe how the land may be employed beyond a single lifetime. Jefferson reasons that if any man or group of men could so control the land—that is, if he or they had a natural right to do anything to or with the land during his or their lifetimes, then he or they could, in effect, "eat up the usufruct of the lands for several generations to come, and then the lands would belong to the dead."[5]

This position, which terminates control over landholdings

not only with the passing of each individual but also with the passing of each generation, is to extend beyond the boundaries of property; it includes the repayment of any debts, public or private, as well as all positive laws—even the Constitution of 1787. Jefferson's principle, then, that "the earth belongs to the living" is precisely what makes his political theory unique; it is, as he puts it, "of very extensive application and consequences."[6] He offers a brief catalog of such applications vis-à-vis France. If they had been implemented by the French, these applications would have turned the traditional world of property holdings on its head, according to Jefferson.

> It [the principle] enters into the resolution of the questions Whether the nation may change the descent of lands holden in tail? Whether they may change the appropriation of lands given antiently to the church, to hospitals, colleges, orders of chivalry, and otherwise in perpetuity? Whether they may abolish the charges and privileges attached on lands, including the whole catalogue ecclesiastical and feudal? It goes to hereditary offices, authorities and jurisdictions; to hereditary orders, distinctions and appellations; to perpetual monopolies in commerce, the arts and sciences; with a long train of et ceteras: and it renders the question of reimbursement a question of generosity and not of right.[7]

Lest the full impact of his principle be misread, he poses the following hypothetical case as a further example. What would be the obligation of the present generation of Frenchmen if Louis XIV and Louis XV had contracted ten thousand Swiss milliards of debt on behalf of the nation? Would either the lands or the revenues from them be due to the creditors? He responds negatively. Realizing that this notion flies in the face of tradition and the "common sense" of the day, Jefferson states that the payment of debts by succeeding generations is a matter of "generosity and not of right." It also follows that if the nation decides to end "perpetual monopolies," compensation is similarly a matter of generosity. A fiscal conservative, Jefferson thought his principle a way of avoiding the crippling accruement of large national debts, which are usually incurred as the result of war. Each generation is responsible for its own monetary matters; if one generation contracts debts which it cannot pay, the succeeding generation (calculated by Jefferson on the basis of mortality tables to evolve every nineteen years) is under no compulsion to do so.[8] Furthermore, by making this principle public policy (i.e., known to the world), both borrowers and lenders are liable either for observing these rules or for paying the consequences.

In the nineteenth year, automatic termination applies to all of the laws and constitutions of society. Quite simply, this means that approximately every twenty years, if not more often, society must reaffirm or construct anew all of its statutes and institutions. The doctrine of tacit consent, made popular by John Locke, may suffice for Publius, author of *The Federalist*, but it will not do for Jefferson. He wants to institutionalize revolution in order to keep the Spirit of 1776 perpetually alive. By this bold innovation, he hopes, first, to sustain every man's interest in governing himself, as opposed to being either politically and economically ruled from the grave or being governed by a permanent aristocracy; and second, to keep the positive laws of society in harmony with the evolutionary progress of man.[9] He makes this second point most brilliantly in a famous 1816 letter to Samuel Kercheval:

> But I know also, that laws and institutions must go hand in hand with the progress of the human mind. As that becomes more developed, more enlightened, as new discoveries are made, new truths disclosed, and manners and opinions change with the change of circumstances, institutions must advance also, and keep pace with the times. We might as well require a man to wear still the coat which fitted him when a boy, as civilized society to remain ever under the regimen of their barbarous ancestors.[10]

In the letter to Madison, early in 1789, the language is different, but the meaning is the same:

> On similar ground it may be proved that no society can make a perpetual constitution, or even a perpetual law. The earth

22

belongs always to the living generation. They may manage it then, and what proceeds from it, as they please, during their usufruct. They are masters too of their own persons, and consequently may govern them as they please. But persons and property make the sum of the objects of government. The constitution and the laws of their predecessors extinguished then in their natural course with those who gave them being. This could preserve that being till it ceased to be itself, and no longer. Every constitution then, and every law, naturally expires at the end of 19 years. If it be enforced longer, it is an act of force, and not of right.[11]

As man progresses, individually and collectively, it is essential for laws to keep pace; by requiring periodic, critical reevaluations of every facet of society, Jefferson believes he can maintain the vitality of a democratic community based on right, not on force.

The 1789 letter to Madison was but the first in a series of similar letters by Jefferson to other friends.[12] Madison's cool and critical reply is of special interest in that it symbolically represents the relationship between the two men. That Jefferson selects Madison to whom to broach his new theory first indeed testifies to the high esteem and warm, fraternal regard that Jefferson had for him; and yet, Madison's polite disapproval—which appears to have had little effect on Jefferson since he continued to advance his position in unaltered form—attests to the acute variances in their political theories.

Claiming that he supports Jefferson's system "in theory," Madison still offers three objections: first, it is impractical, subjecting the society to the uncertainties of an "interregnum"; second, "*improvements* made by the dead form a debt against the living who take the benefit of them"; and third, unless special prohibitory provisions are enacted, "pernicious factions" will challenge the existing property laws, thus resulting in depreciation in their value. Madison also suggests that "*tacit* assent" can serve Jefferson's purposes without placing society in the precarious situation of being perpetually in transition.[13] But perpetual transition is precisely what Jefferson wants.

Given Madison's concept of man, which views him as an atomized unit of perpetual motion who inevitably joins a faction which, more often than not, is at odds with some other faction in society, his first objection to Jefferson's theory is understandable: unlike Jefferson, who sees society as natural, Madison fails to see any other reason for men forming civil society than a sort of Hobbesian prudence.[14] Madison's second and third criticisms of Jefferson's idea are closely linked together; they evoke numerous practical considerations which Madison feels Jefferson has overlooked. If succeeding generations are not obligated to repay the debts of the present, who is? What happens to property? Who will loan capital if repayment beyond a lifetime is not assured? Without *"tacit* assent" can you have any civil society at all?

On this specific proposition, then, the "Great Collaborators" are miles apart.[15] Where Jefferson wants to initiate a theoretical dialogue concerning the optimum method to ensure the possibility for the happiness, harmony, and autonomy of succeeding generations, Madison only wants to be practical. And so, rather than even enter into speculative discourse, he elects to quibble. As will become clear, the differences between these Founding Fathers extend beyond the confines of this single letter; the schism is the logical outgrowth of their divergent concepts of man and society and about the fulfillment of both.

Prior to Jefferson's explicitly rejecting property as a natural right, this position can be inferred not only from his private letters but also from his public works. In an early paper called "A Summary View of the Rights of British Americans," written two years prior to the Declaration of Independence, Jefferson, in contrast to the Declaration, shows tremendous concern over questions of property.[16] In polite but firm language, he informs the king of the relationship between property and labor. "America was conquered, and her settlements made and firmly established," writes Jefferson, "at the expence of individuals, and not of the British public." Resolutely, Jefferson points out that the colonists' "own blood was spilt" and "their own fortunes expended" in the establishment of the colonies; all of their labor, moreover, was "for themselves," not for the crown. To Jefferson, the individual's expenditure of his energy, his labor, and his blood gives him civil property rights that an English sovereign cannot invade. This is an important point. Jefferson is not arguing that there is a natural right to property, even though he does believe in natural rights. In the "Summary View," free trade and expatriation are expressly placed in the category of natural right.[17] By expatriating themselves from England, Jefferson argues, the colonists automatically have the right to establish their own positive laws regarding property, or regarding anything else not reserved to man. With these laws neither the king nor Parliament may rightly tamper. Certain other property questions between the Colonies and England are resolved by Jefferson in this treatise.

The king claimed that the Colonies were his landholdings, with the relationship between the owner and the user of property being feudal in nature. Had this claim been legitimate, Jefferson's objections to interference would not have been justified. Jefferson counters that the holdings are allodial and therefore that the king possesses no right to control. How did this discrepancy over the nature of the holdings originate? Jefferson explains: "Our ancestors however, who migrated hither, were laborers, not lawyers. The fictitious principle that all lands belong originally to the king, they were early persuaded to believe real, and accordingly took grants of their own lands from the crown." As long as the Royal price of land was low, the colonists had few objections. By the early 1770s the price of property was increasing; as a result, Jefferson believed, albeit unfoundedly, that a decrease in immigration was threatening the growth of the New World. And so, as a "laborer" and as a lawyer, Jefferson takes it upon himself to set the record straight:

> It is time therefore for us to lay this matter before his majesty, and to declare that he has no right to grant lands of himself. From the nature and purpose of civil institutions, all the lands

within the limits which any particular society has circum-
scribed around itself, are assumed by that society, and
subject to their allotment only. This may be done by themselves assembled collectively, or by their legislature to whom
they may have delegated sovereign authority: and, if they are
allotted in neither of these ways, each individual of the
society may appropriate to himself such lands as he finds
vacant, and occupancy will give him title.[18]

Jefferson believes that coincident with the creation of civil
society, property rights are created.[19] Insofar as the Colonies
are composed of separate sovereign societies, each has a
right to govern itself in terms of property usage. The king of
England, therefore, has no right—civil, feudal, or natural—to
interfere in these internal relationships.

Two years later, in the Declaration of Independence,
Jefferson characteristically opens with additional "self-evident" truths: "that all men are created equal, that they are
endowed by their Creator with certain unalienable Rights,
that among these are Life, Liberty and the pursuit of
Happiness."[20] Nowhere in the critical opening paragraphs
does Jefferson use the term *property*. A concept that is less
definitive and more encompassing than the usual property
terminology of Jefferson's age, *happiness* is the end of government and of man's endeavors. Although it can be argued
that all reasonable men of that era assumed that property
was a necessary (and perhaps sufficient) prerequisite to life,
liberty, and the pursuit of happiness, that Jefferson did not
use the word is historically novel. Moreover, as will become
clear later, property ownership per se was not considered by
Jefferson to be an end in itself. Man was meant to be much
more than either a mere consumer or an appropriator. Not
surprisingly, it is only in the twenty-first paragraph that the
term *property*, for the first and last time, explicitly appears.
The noted Jefferson scholar Adrienne Koch claims that there
is nothing extraordinary in the choice of words used above,
because Jefferson was striving for "moral, humane, and
eloquent symbols . . . [in his] manifesto that was expected to
mobilize the thirteen colonies for war."[21]

26

True as this may be, the fact cannot be easily overlooked that Jefferson rejects the traditional Lockean triad of "life, liberty, and estate." The omission is significant. While Locke views property as a natural right and its accumulation as the fulfillment of human endeavors, Jefferson does not. Jefferson's vision of man and of man's *telos* is much grander. Happiness is the *summum bonum*. More importantly, every man has a natural right to pursue it.[22] Property is merely an institution created by society to help men gain "life, liberty, and the pursuit of happiness." Hence, property laws should be altered at least every nineteen years in order to ensure this goal.

Politically, Jefferson struggled to change the property laws in his home state of Virginia by drafting legislation that would put an end to the last feudal holdovers of entail and primogeniture.[23] Entail and primogeniture guaranteed that the eldest son would inherit the father's estate *in toto*, and thus perpetuated large landholdings. Inequality of property is viewed by Jefferson as the root of "numberless instances of wretchedness." Everything that is "practicable" must be done to equalize property relations. He writes to the Reverend James Madison:

> I am conscious that an equal division of property is impractable. But the consequences of this enormous inequality producing so much misery to the bulk of mankind, legislators cannot invent too many devices for subdividing property, only taking care to let their subdivisions go hand in hand with the natural affections of the human mind.

He notes the impracticality, not the impropriety, of equality. Although he does not believe that it is politically possible to redistribute property equally, he does argue that every male must be given some amount of property, at least fifty acres, in order to live. As the next chapter makes clear, in a sense Jefferson argues for equality insofar as all members of society own enough land to provide for life, liberty, and the pursuit of happiness. In the letter to Madison, he puts it this way:

> Whenever there is in any country, uncultivated lands and unemployed poor, it is clear that the laws of property have

27

been so far extended as to violate natural right. The earth is
given as a common stock for man to labour and live on. If, for
the encouragement of industry we allow it to be appropriated, we must take care that other employment be furnished
to those excluded from the appropriation. If we do not the
fundamental right to labour the earth returns to the unemployed.[24]

On the basis of this letter, Charles Wiltse concludes that in
Jefferson's political theory can be found an "organic conception of society," in opposition to Locke's individualism.[25]
Progressive taxation is an additional technique that Jefferson
believes will help to redistribute wealth and ought to be
employed before the rot sets in.

Jefferson drops the old Lockean property terminology on
at least one other significant occasion. While serving as the
United States minister to France, he stood at the center of the
reform movement there. When asked by Lafayette to review
the *Déclaration des droits de l'homme*, Jefferson bracketed the
words *"droit à la propriété"* and appears to have urged
Lafayette to substitute the phrase *"la recherche du bonheur."*[26]
Once again, happiness is what Jefferson believes ought to be
the concern of man; it is *bonheur*, not *propriété*, to which all
men have an equal, natural right.

The implications of every man's possessing a natural right
to life, liberty, and the pursuit of happiness, with property as
merely an instrumental civil right, are staggering. Adrienne
Koch sees the obvious implications of this position but fails
to pursue them: "While Jefferson recognized that the right
to property could be alienated by society, or varied indefi-
nitely by the specific civil laws of society, he believed that the
natural right to the means of subsistence should restrain the
nature of those civil laws."[27] Where Koch is either timid or
blind, refusing to push to its logical conclusion the idea of a
"natural right to the means of subsistence," other scholars
are not. Staughton Lynd, for instance, maintains that in
Jefferson's principle of "the earth belongs to the living," the
American Revolution "approached most nearly the socialist
conception that living labor has claims superior to any

property rights." And although neither Jefferson nor any other person of the Revolutionary era ever pushed this argument to the conclusion reached by Marx, early-nineteenth-century American socialists built upon it.[28] Still, before proceeding to these further considerations, a more complete discussion of land and farming is apropos.

3
Political Economy:
Land, Liberty, and Leisure

I am savage enough to prefer the woods, the wilds, and the independence of Monticello, to all the brilliant pleasures of this gay capital. I shall therefore rejoin myself to my native country with new attachments, with exaggerated esteem for its advantages, for tho' there is less wealth there, there is more freedom, more ease and less misery.[1]

—Jefferson

Even though there is no natural right to property in his political theory, Jefferson perceives direct relationships between individual freedom, economic autonomy, and democratic community. Here is where the small, independent farmer enters into Jefferson's vision of the good life.

As a result of his stay in Europe, Jefferson acquired firsthand knowledge of the unhealthy effects that a possessive market society had on those men who had no choice but to toil as wage laborers.[2] These effects can be poignantly seen in a note to John Adams, wherein Jefferson contrasts the enviable economic position of the United States—with its free land—to that of Europe. Rather than risk the loss of the full tenor and impact of this section of the letter, I quote from it at length.

Before the establishment of the American states, nothing was known to History but the Man of the old world, crouded within limits either small or overcharged, and steeped in the vices which that situation generates. A government adapted to such men would be one thing; but a very different one than for the Man of these states. Here every one may have land to labor for himself if he chuses; or, preferring the exercise of any other industry, may exact for it such compensation as not only to afford a comfortable subsistence, but

31

wherewith to provide for a cessation from labor in old age. Every one, by his property, or by his satisfactory situation, is interested in the support of law and order. And such men may safely and advantageously reserve to themselves a wholsome controul over their public affairs, and a degree of freedom, which in the hands of the *Canaille* of the cities of Europe, would be instantly perverted to the demolition and destruction of every thing public and private.[3]

As long as land is available, there is no economic dependence; as long as the laborer has the option of meeting his needs on his own land, he can freely choose to leave the land and enter a wage-labor situation that is not automatically based on exploitation: that is, a wage-labor relationship in which the laborer "may extract" for his services "such compensation" as to "afford a comfortable subsistence." In this sense, then, the American laborer, unlike his European counterpart, could achieve a significant degree of economic freedom.

Thomas Paine also observes the inherently exploitative nature of wage-labor relationships in a market economy, and he, too, connects it with the bourgeois institution of property.

> Separate an individual from society, and give him an island or a continent to possess, and he cannot acquire personal property. He cannot be rich. . . . All accumulation, therefore, of personal property, beyond what a man's own hands produce, is derived to him by living in society; and he owes on every principle of justice, of gratitude, and of civilization, a part of that accumulation back again to society from whence the whole came.
>
> This is putting the matter on a general principle, and perhaps it is best to do so; for if we examine the case minutely it will be found that the accumulation of personal property is, in many instances, the effect of paying too little for the labor that produced it; the consequence of which is that the working hand perishes in old age, and the employer abounds in affluence.[4]

When the land in a society becomes monopolized, it is possible for one class to pay "too little" to another class for

32

labor, since those without property must work for those with property, or they will starve. Writing for a different economic situation, in which land was already scarce, Paine proposes different political remedies from Jefferson's in order to cope with the unjust distribution of wealth and power.

His argument in *Agrarian Justice* begins with the principle "that the condition of every person born into the world, after a state of civilization commences, ought not to be worse than if he had been born before that period." Since the earth originally was *"the common property of the human race,"* everyone would have possessed some property. But the earth, in this uncultivated condition, could not support a large number of inhabitants; with the invention of private property, major improvement in productivity develops. While the cultivated land is more bountiful, the social system it generates renders as much as half of the inhabitants of the country propertyless and destitute. The liberal Paine has a problem: he cannot take away the property of those who labored upon it, even if the propertyless have, in a sense, been dispossessed of their inheritance. To ameliorate this injustice, Paine argues for the creation of a national fund. The fund would be supplied by the proprietors who owe the community a *"ground-rent"* from the profits they make on the land and from a 10 percent inheritance tax.[5] As a matter of "right, and not a charity," every person at the age of twenty-one, regardless of economic status, receives "fifteen pounds sterling, as a compensation in part, for the loss of his or her natural inheritance"; and every person, upon reaching the age of fifty, is entitled to "the sum of ten pounds per annum."[6] Although Paine remains trapped in the bourgeois world view of property, his proposals to remedy social injustice were radical for this era and, in time, would become the basis of socialist demands. Still, Paine appears to have a greater respect for and a greater reluctance to tamper with property than has Jefferson, who seems to be willing to redistribute property with every generation and urges legislators to "invent" as many devices as possible to keep property equal.

Though relatively equal degrees of property ownership were always important to economic freedom, in another more meaningful sense, differences in the quality of life provided by the divergent working environments of the urban, as opposed to the rural, setting were so disproportionately in favor of the latter that Jefferson was positive that the majority of Americans would freely choose the life of the husbandman over that of the industrial laborer. Even a "manufacturer" who had been transplanted from Europe to the New World would find himself, proclaims Jefferson, "irresistibly tempted by the independence" of living in a small farm community, surrounded by his wife, his family, and his friends; he would, consequently, readily abandon his old vocation in exchange for a new style of life.[7] In this passage, then, Jefferson clearly demonstrates that he believes that there is an intimate relationship between men and their environment. Rather than maintain that there is but one model of man, based on some fixed, immutable laws of human behavior, Jefferson believes that man's nature changes under the impact of time, as well as of circumstances. A laborer, raised in the dark decadence of a European factory, may join in the urban mobs of oppression, but this same laborer also has the potential to be a virtuous citizen if he is placed securely in the bosom of the bountiful and beautiful Virginia Commonwealth.

Jefferson's acute understanding of the relationship between circumstances and men shows clearly in his recollections of Paris. While past political theories—for example, those of Hobbes and Locke—had been based on a particular model of man who was the result of a particular type of society, "crowded within limits either small or over charged, and steeped in the vices which that situation generates," the New World, with its simple market society, provides Americans with the opportunity of living together harmoniously, without becoming "embraced" by the possessive individualism of the full market society of Europe.[8]

Given this need for economic freedom as a basis for a democratic society, it is logical that Jefferson first attempts to incorporate it politically into his home state of Virginia. The discussion in the previous chapter of Jefferson's principle that the earth belongs to the living is part of that plan. In addition, in all three versions of his proposed model constitutions for the state of Virginia, fifty acres of land are to be given to every male who does not already own that much property. In one of the draft constitutions, this grant assures the citizen not only of economic but also of political freedom in that the right of suffrage is tied to the ownership of property.[9] To Jefferson, economics and politics are always contingent upon each other. To talk of them as separate realms makes no sense. Hence, true freedom in the one area necessitates freedom in the other.

The relationship between economics and politics extends to a macroscopic plane.[10] If men become possessed by the blind pursuit of profit, rather than by the Jeffersonian virtues of freedom, friendship, and felicity, they will unknowingly bring about their own demise. This foreboding is present in his *Notes on the State of Virginia:*

> From the conclusion of this war we shall be going down hill. It will not then be necessary to resort every moment to the people for support. They will be forgotten, therefore, and their rights disregarded. They will forget themselves, but in the sole faculty of making money, and will never think of uniting to effect a due respect for their rights. The shackles, therefore, which shall not be knocked off at the conclusion of this war, will remain on us long, will be made heavier and heavier, till our rights shall revive or expire in a convulsion.[11]

In a private letter written during the same time, Jefferson conveys a sense of "despair" that he is experiencing because of the tendencies of Americans to be persuaded by "fashion and folly" to purchase, on credit, every "gewgaw held out."[12] Credit, in every form, spells ruin to Jefferson. Neither governments nor societies nor individuals should be permitted to buy on credit: the short-term gains result in long-term, often fatal losses: "Every discouragement should be thrown in the way of men who undertake to trade without capital."[13] A year later, in 1786, he suggests: "As it

35

is impossible to prevent credit, the best way would be to cure it's ill effects by giving an instantaneous recovery to the creditor. This would be reducing purchases on credit to purchases for ready money."[14] As for the society as a corporate body, Jefferson believes that his doctrine of "the earth belongs to the living" can act as a suitable check on fiscal extravagance. Because his principle has never been implemented, the specter of the necessity of choosing between luxury and autonomy continues to haunt him. In 1816 he recalls these stark images he has presented in his *Notes* as he cautions against public debts:

> We must make our election between *economy and liberty*, or *profusion and servitude*. If we run into such debts, as that we must be taxed in our meat and in our drink, in our necessaries and our comforts, in our labors and our amusements, for our callings and our creeds, as the people of England are, our people, like them, must come to labor sixteen hours in the twenty-four, give the earnings of fifteen of these to the government for their debts and daily expenses; and the sixteenth being insufficient to afford us bread, we must live, as they now do, on oatmeal and potatoes; have no time to think, no means of calling the mismanagers to account; but be glad to obtain subsistence by hiring ourselves to rivet their chains on the necks of our fellow-sufferers.[15]

This quotation begins to get at the nub of one of the central features of Jefferson's philosophy. Many political theorists who wrote during the historic period from the sixteenth to at least the first quarter of the nineteenth century were attempting to construct formal rules and institutions for an emerging market society. Their design would allow men the opportunity to pursue their own narrowly constructed self-interest, which was itself defined by the society, within the confines of a social structure that limited and channeled human behavior, so that the whole would thus be stable and provide an environment conducive for the creation of *The Wealth of Nations*. In his *Fable of the Bees*, Bernard Mandeville succinctly captures the image: "Thus every part was full of vice, yet the whole mass a paradise." Jefferson rejects this sort of "ideal" altogether. His world view is founded on a different concept of man and a different notion of society; it is a world view shaped, formed, and colored by a distinctly nonmarket ethos.[16] Macroeconomic and microeconomic matters are important only insofar as they influence the development of man and society. The mentality of Monticello is not based on debits and credits, but on freedom, friendship, and felicity. Society, moreover, has the right to attempt to legislate this ethos, insofar as possible. Jefferson leaves little doubt that this is his intent in an 1816 letter:

> Every society has a right to fix the fundamental principles of its association, and to say to all individuals, that, if they contemplate pursuits beyond the limits of these principles, and involving dangers which the society chooses to avoid, they must go somewhere else for their exercise; that we want no citizens, and still less ephemeral and pseudo-citizens, on such terms. We may exclude them from our territory, as we do persons infected with disease. Such is the situation of our country. We have most abundant resources of happiness within ourselves, which we may enjoy in peace and safety, without permitting a few citizens, infected with the mania of rambling and gambling, to bring danger on the great mass engaged in innocent and safe pursuits at home. In your letter to Fisk, you have fairly stated the alternatives between which we are to choose: 1, licentious commerce and gambling speculations for a few, with eternal war for the many; or, 2, restricted commerce, peace, and steady occupations for all. If any State in the Union will declare that it prefers separation with the first alternative, to a continuance in union without it, I have no hesitation in saying, "let us separate." I would rather the States should withdraw, which are for unlimited commerce and war, and confederate with those alone which are for peace and agriculture.[17]

If the commercial Northeast desires an economic existence so divergent from that of Virginia that it threatens the pastoral life style of Jefferson's dream, then disunion, separation, and friendly isolation are the remedies. Moderation, peace, and community are goals that he will not give up, as can be seen in his private correspondence. As early as 1784, he is already urging his friend James Madison to purchase land near Monticello so that he may join James Monroe and William Short to form a "partie quarree." This occurrence, writes Jefferson, will again convince him that life holds additional happiness in store for him, because "agreeable society is the first essential in constituting the happiness and of course the value of our existence." He terminates his plea by advising Madison to "weigh well the value of this against the difference in pecuniary interest, and ask yourself which will add most to the sum of your felicity through life." Not one lacking in self-confidence, he communicates to Madison the preordained result: "I think that weighing them in this balance, your decision will be favourable to all our prayers."[18] An extended discussion of Jefferson's response to "Query XIX" in his *Notes on the State of Virginia* will bring this nonmarket, nonmaterial ethos into even sharper focus.

"Manufacturing" is the title of this keystone chapter in *Notes on the State of Virginia*. He uses this brief exposition to paint a vivid black-on-white panorama of the critical differences between Europe and America. This contrast is deeply etched in Jefferson's mind; throughout his writings it resurfaces, often in the form of a juxtaposition of artisan versus farmer or urban versus rural setting. In each instance the picture is presented as a near-cosmic struggle between good and evil.

The opening paragraph to Query XIX is straightforward. It analytically describes the current state of manufacturers in Virginia, which is to say that they are of minor value in this rural commonwealth. The first part of the second paragraph continues in the same scientific tone, as it proceeds to raise an issue that Jefferson is anxious to expound upon.

"The political oeconomists of Europe have established it as a principle that every state should endeavour to manufacture for itself: and this principle, like many others, we transfer to America, without calculating the difference of circumstance which should often produce a difference of result." As usual, he finds the unique circumstances of each continent of significant variation: "In Europe the lands are either cultivated, or locked up against the cultivator. Manufacture must therefore be resorted to of necessity not of choice."[19] Economic freedom is clearly the concern here. Americans have it; Europeans do not. But the issue is even more important than that. It is a question of the quality of life. The rural experience is unique. It allows the individual to have control over his destiny while pursuing happiness in a bucolic, aesthetic locale. So great are the chances of men finding human fulfillment in a farm environment that Jefferson believes that no effort ought to be spared in providing all men with the opportunity for such a life. In the 1780s he passionately believes that manufacturing cannot provide a similar reward. At this point in Query XIX, dropping all pretense of being a dispassionate observer, Jefferson poses a rhetorical question: "Is it best then that all our citizens should be employed in its improvement, or that one half should be called off from that to exercise manufactures and handicraft arts for the other?" At its mythopoeic best, the response is pure Jefferson:

> Those who labour in the earth are the chosen people of God, if ever he had a chosen people, whose breasts he has made his peculiar deposit for substantial and genuine virtue. It is the focus in which he keeps alive that sacred fire, which otherwise might escape from the face of the earth. Corruption of morals in the mass of cultivators is a phaenomenon of which no age nor nation has furnished an example. It is the mark set on those, who not looking up to heaven, to their own soil and industry, as does the husbandman, for their subsistance, depend for it on the casualties and caprice of customers. Dependance begets subservience and venality, suffocates the germ of virtue, and prepares fit tools for the designs of ambition. This, the natural progress and consequence of the arts, has sometimes perhaps been retarded by accidental circumstances: but, generally speaking, the proportion which the aggregate of the other classes of citizens bears in any state to that of its husbandmen, is the proportion of its unsound to its healthy parts, and is a good-enough barometer whereby to measure its degree of corruption.[20]

"Substantial and genuine virtue" is the attribute of the

farmer. Morality, not profitability, is the criterion for judgment. With the ready availability of free land, the option of selecting between manufacturing and farming is not a real choice. The steady, wholesome employment of the husbandman is much more conducive to human fulfillment than is service that is dependent "on the casualties and caprice of customers." Jefferson hopes, perhaps naïvely, to exclude forever the spirit of the possessive market from America. Writing to George Washington in 1787, he notes that "the wealth acquired by speculation and plunder is fugacious in it's nature and fills society with the spirit of gambling. The moderate and sure income of husbandry begets permanent improvement, quiet life, and orderly conduct."[21] And in 1792, again commenting on the "gambling" mentality that was on the rise because of the success of banking, he disapproves of the fact that

> the bank has just now notified it's proprietors that they may call for a dividend of 10. per cent on their capital for the last 6. months. This makes a profit of 26. per cent per annum. Agriculture, commerce, & every thing *useful* must be neglected, when the *useless* employment of money is so much more lucrative.[22]

Quote on banking

The physiocratic flavor is manifest: agriculture is useful; it creates real value; and yet, men may be tempted by the glitter of gold. It becomes the responsibility of legislators, then, to divert men's eyes through institutions, laws, and education.

It is possible to accuse Jefferson of wanting to erect his ideal society upon a slave foundation as its basis: not the slavery of the American black, but the wage slavery of European laborers. "Let our work-shops remain in Europe," he admonishes. "It is better to carry provisions and materials to workmen there, than bring them to the provisions and materials, and with them their manners and principles."[23] The virgin setting must not be soiled with the social disease of industrialized Europe. His answer to Query XIX ends with this exhortation: "The mobs of great cities add just so much to the support of pure government, as sores do to the strength of the human body. It is the manners and spirit of a people which preserve a republic in vigour. A degeneracy in these is a canker which soon eats to the heart of its laws and constitution.''[24]

If Query XIX leaves any room for doubt about Jefferson's jaundiced perception of the deplorable condition of Europe, his 1785 epistle to Charles Bellini alleviates any shadows. ''A savage of the mountains of America,'' Jefferson wants to contrast metaphorically the Old and the New worlds. The comparison reaches almost exactly the opposite conclusion to John Locke's. In his *Second Treatise* Locke attempts to show the real advantage of life in England, where farming was subject to the advantages of private property and enclosure, compared to those societies which were still in a primitive state of nature, in which property was held in common, as among the American Indians:

> There cannot be a clearer demonstration of any thing, than several Nations of the *Americans* are of this, who are rich in Land, and poor in all the Comforts of Life; whom Nature having furnished as liberally as any other people, with the materials of Plenty, i.e. a fruitful Soil, apt to produce in abundance, what might serve for food, rayment, and delight; yet for want of improving it by labour, have not one hundreth part of the Conveniences we enjoy: And a King of a large fruitful Territory there feeds, lodges, and is clad worse than a day Labourer in *England*.[25]

From Locke's perspective, those men on the bottom of the social structure of England are, at least materially, better off than those at the zenith in the New World. John Locke never visited the colonies; his conclusions about life there are based on secondary reports. After Jefferson has been in Europe for some time and has directly viewed the conditions of its people, he comes to conclusions opposite to those of Locke:

> I find the general fate of humanity here most deplorable. The truth of Voltaire's observation offers itself perpetually, that every man here must be either the hammer or the anvil. It is a true picture of that country to which they say we shall pass

hereafter, and where we are to see god and his angels in splendor, and crouds of the damned trampled under their feet. While the great mass of the people are thus suffering under physical and moral oppression, I have endeavored to examine more nearly the condition of the great, to appreciate the true value of the circumstances in their situation which dazzle the bulk of the spectators, and especially to compare it with that degree of happiness which is enjoyed in America by every class of people.[26]

In all such comparisons made by Jefferson, the Americans fare far better than the Europeans. It must be remembered that material conditions are but one facet of his evaluation. In terms of "conjugal love" and "domestic happiness," which are more important in Jefferson's good society than wealth or trade, the Europeans are hopelessly lacking; as for scientific knowledge, while it is true that the European "literati" are "half a dozen years" ahead of the Americans, Jefferson nevertheless believes that "the mass of [Europe's] people is two centuries behind ours." Wherever he turns, Jefferson's scale always tilts in favor of the New World, with its rural, natural environment. What, if anything, does Europe have to offer? From the Old World, Jefferson wishes his "countrymen to adopt just so much of European politeness as to be ready (to) make all those little sacrifices of self which really render European manners amiable, and relieve society from the disagreeable scenes to which rudeness often exposes it."[27] However, beyond these rudiments of social etiquette, Europe has little of positive worth to give America: except, of course, its constant posture as a counterexample of a style of existence into which Americans will inevitably fall if they, too, become dominated by the pursuit of money, vanity, prestige, or power, rather than by *la recherche du bonheur*.

Several additional points must be made with regard to Query XIX. To begin with, Jefferson's poetic response shows him to be too grandiose a figure to be contained within the limits of agrarianism pure and simple.[28] In his answer to the question, he astonishingly shifts from the sparse, arid, and analytic language of political economy to a figurativ̶e̶, ̶.̶.̶.̶ opoeic language in order to capture more adequately his image of a democratic society of free and virtuous husbandmen. This Jeffersonian vision of the good life, its roots dating back at least as far as Vergil, has been appropriately called "pastoral" by Leo Marx in his captivating and now largely ignored study of the pastoral ideal in American history. More importantly, this pastoral metaphor pulls Jefferson out from under limits of the narrower agrarian model of his day. Leo Marx explains this critical difference thus:

> Although the term *agrarian* ordinarily is used to describe the social ideal that Jefferson is endorsing here, to call it *pastoral* would be more accurate and illuminating. This is not a quibble: a serious distinction is involved. To begin with, the astonishing shift from the spare language of political economics to a highly figurative, mythopoeic language indicates that Jefferson is adopting a literary point of view; or, to be more exact, he is adopting a point of view for which an accepted literary convention is available. . . .
>
> What, then, is the difference? The chief difference is the relative importance of economic factors implied by each term. To call Jefferson an agrarian is to imply that his argument rests, at bottom, upon a commitment to an agricultural economy. But in Query XIX he manifestly is repudiating the importance of economic criteria in evaluating the relative merits of various forms of society. Although the true agrarians of his day, the physiocrats, had demonstrated the superior efficiency of large-scale agriculture, Jefferson continues to advocate the small, family-sized farm.[29]

Jefferson, in Query XIX, implicitly rejects the relevance of economic criteria in evaluating the merits of various forms of society. Although many of his physiocratic friends had long advocated the economic advantages of large-scale farming, Jefferson remains adamant in his fidelity to small, family farming. Monticello becomes the symbol of the good life: each person is a member both of a family and of a community and yet is an individual all the same. If one extends Monticello across the surrounding countryside and adds the ward-republics (to be discussed later), an environment conducive to "social love" and harmony is present.[30] It is, after all, "virtue," "freedom," and "happiness," not economic "profusion," for which he longs.

These sentiments, favoring the industry of farming over any other activity, are not isolated moments in the thoughts of Jefferson. His writings are peppered with phrases and paragraphs that sing the virtues of the life of the husbandman. In other sections of his *Notes on the State of Virginia*, in conformity with his desire to keep the "workshops" (and corruption) in Europe, Jefferson advocates that America abandon the oceans to Europe. He would like "to leave [it] to others to bring what we shall want, and to carry what we can spare. This would make us invulnerable to Europe . . . and would turn all our citizens to the cultivation of the earth; and, I repeat it again, cultivators of the earth are the most virtuous and independent citizens."[31]

In a letter to two young gentlemen who are about to undertake a journey to Europe, Jefferson offers some advice on sights that "an American" would want to investigate. Indeed, the recommended tour is almost a carbon copy of Jefferson's own 1787 selection of sights that were worthy of his own inspection. Writing to his aide, William Short, he explains that he has "not visited at all the manufactures of this place: because a knowledge of them would be useless, and would extrude from the memory other things more worth retaining. Architecture, painting, sculpture, antiquities, agriculture, the condition of the labouring poor fill all my moments."[32] Under the heading "Objects of attention for an American," he first and foremost recommends to his acquaintances the study of agriculture, with the view of observing what "might be transported to America." As for the "mechanical arts, and manufactures," Jefferson admits that "some . . . will be worth a superficial view," but he thinks that it "would be a waste of attention to examine these minutely." Although it would be "a waste" to review the "mechanical arts," Jefferson does urge his readers to

take every possible occasion for entering into the hovels of the labourers, and especially at the moments of their repast, see what they eat, how they are cloathed, whether they are obliged to labour too hard; whether the government or their landlord takes from them an unjust proportion of their labour; on what footing stands the property they call their own, their personal liberty &c.[33]

At the conclusion of such an experience, Jefferson is sure that he will have at least two additional converts to the pastoral cause. Still, he would prefer that American youths stay at home, safely removed from the multiple forms of European seduction, to which the young are readily tempted.[34] As for the mature American like himself, the effect of the grand tour will be beneficial because it will root the traveler's love of home all the more firmly as the contrast between virtue and vice becomes self-evident.

Jefferson's advice points to yet-another aspect of his pastoralism. As is well known, Jefferson's personal "trinity" was composed of Bacon, Newton, and Locke.[35] Of especial influence on him was Locke's *Essay Concerning Human Understanding*—not the *Second Treatise*, which is all too often mistakenly assumed to be the primary Lockean influence on him.[36] Setting out to discover the limits to human knowledge, in the first three chapters of this work, Locke concludes that there are "No Innate Principles in the Mind" and "No Innate Practical Principles." Nonetheless, he believes that moral principles can be worked out on the basis of utility. All knowledge, then, comes from experience. Man is like "white paper" upon which almost anything may be written. A child, similarly, "is wax to be fashioned and molded as one pleases."[37] Although Locke never appeared to push his theory to its logical conclusions, in later theorists these notions take on extraordinary implications: since all that men are comes from experience, differences between them must be based on differences in environment: alter men's environment and education, and they can be good.[38] Hence, François Fourier looks forward to a France that will be inhabited by thirty million scientists like Newton and thirty million poets like Shakespeare.[39] In Jefferson, the manifestations of Locke's psychology are analogous. If men are placed in the overcrowded, decadent black holes of European cities, they will indeed become beasts. But if they are placed in a bucolic, aesthetic, bountiful pastoral setting, where they are free to do as they please, free to work and play with nature, their innate sociability will not be suppressed, but rather will flower.[40]

In his *Notes on the State of Virginia* Jefferson further demonstrates his concern with pastoralism beyond simple agrarianism when he discusses the "infinite wretchedness" of the cultivation of tobacco: "Those employed in it are in a continued state of exertion beyond the powers of nature to support. Little food of any kind is raised by them; so that the men and animals on these farms are badly fed, and the earth is rapidly impoverished." It must be recalled that the land was given in usufruct; therefore, ecological damage must be avoided wherever possible. He then contrasts this state of affairs with that of wheat farming. "The cultivation of wheat is the reverse [of tobacco] in every circumstance. Besides cloathing the earth with herbage, and preserving its fertility, it feeds the labourers plentifully, requires from them only a moderate toil, . . . and diffuses plenty and happiness among the whole."[41] Clearly, this latter style of farming is what sparked the Jeffersonian imagination.

Along this same vein, Jefferson, like the Francis Bacon of his trinity, is anxious to start a "System of Agricultural Societies," the purpose of which is "to promote . . . the diffusion of this skill, and thereby to procure, with the same labor now employed, greater means of subsistence and of happiness to our fellow citizens."[42] An early proponent of "Small Is Beautiful," Jefferson tries to introduce decentralization into virtually every facet of life; not wishing to see these scientific agricultural societies centrally controlled from the federal capital, he persuasively argues for local jurisdiction.[43]

Unsurprisingly, albeit with tragic results, Jefferson attempted to introduce agriculture to the Indian nations within America in the hopes of improving their condition.[44] It is possible to select from many of Jefferson's messages to the various Indian tribes and to find this recurring th little land well stocked and improved, will yield more than a great deal without stock or improvement." "We shall be pleased to see you making progress in raising stock and grain. . . . A little labor in this way, performed at home and at ease, will go further towards feeding and clothing you, than a great deal of labor in hunting wild beasts." "A little land, and a little labor, will procure more provisions than the most successful hunt."[45] All of these are examples of Jefferson's concern not just with farming but also with a scientific farming that will free men from endless toil.

So, no matter where one turns in Jefferson's writings on political economy, it is obvious that he longs for a scientific farm community, hoping thus to produce a pastoral America. A "golden mean" environment, between the carefree anarchy of the wilderness and the decadent overcivilization of the urban cesspools, Jefferson's pastoral vision is that of a well-groomed, bountiful garden. He wants every male to have his own piece of land, where he can meet the biological needs of his family and still have sufficient energy at the end of the day "to think."[46] The role of science is to augment man's desire to understand his world and to help liberate him from unnecessary toil.

Jefferson, then, does not advocate farming for the sake of farming: his idea of the good life is not a puritanical picture of endless toil on and with the earth from dawn to dusk, from womb to tomb, thereby leaving the farmer neither time nor energy to fall from grace. Instead, Jefferson seeks a pastoral ideal, a form of scientific farming in which the farmer can take advantage of all the arts of agriculture, where he can be free from the conditions of the wage laborer of Europe, and still have enough energy at the end of the day to cultivate his own private and public interests and concerns. Though this system will result in less wealth in America than in Europe, it will also provide "more freedom, more ease, and less misery."[47] Quite simply, he wants all the benefits of science, technology, and agriculture without any of the costs of industrialization. Several times he entertains the notion that manufacturing should be restricted to the small farms, acting as a buffer against large-scale foreign and domestic industrialization.[48] Indeed, he fancies himself as a "nail-maker," and for a brief period he ran his backyard factory at Monticello profitably.

Although the early pastoral image found in *Notes on the State of Virginia* is agrarian, too often Jefferson is erroneously viewed as being completely against manufacturing. Though he wishes to remain agrarian, Jefferson is usually (sooner or later), a realist. As early as 1791 he is openly endorsing the wisdom of America's gradually moving into manufacturing.[49] By 1801, he is speaking favorably of "the four pillars of our prosperity"—namely, "agriculture, manufactures, commerce, and navigation";[50] in 1809, he trusts that "the good sense" of his countrymen will enable them to see that geopolitical realities are such that their continued autonomy will depend upon "a due balance between agriculture, manufactures and commerce."[51] Agriculture continues to head the list, but manufacturing, commerce, and navigation are now imperative to the cause. With the end of the War of 1812, his steady movement toward manufacturing is complete: the economic circumstances outlined in *Notes on the State of Virginia* have changed radically. Jefferson's vision, therefore, follows suit.

In a letter to Benjamin Austin written in 1816, Jefferson explains the reasons for his change of mind on the subject of manufacturing. He tells Austin that in the final quarter of the eighteenth century, the world politicoeconomic scene was far different from that of the present. At that time the question of agriculture versus manufacture was easily resolved in favor of the former, "on this consideration chiefly, that to the labor of the husbandman a vast addition is made by the spontaneous energies of the earth on which it is employed: for one grain of wheat committed to the earth, she renders twenty, thirty, and even fifty fold, whereas to the labor of the manufacturer nothing is added. Pounds of flax, in his hands, yield, on the contrary, but pennyweights of lace." To Jefferson, nature, not man, is the creator of real value.[52] There is, therefore, an obvious physiocratic bias in favor of farming as opposed to manufacturing, where "nothing is added." And yet, as Jefferson readily points out, "who in 1785 could foresee the rapid depravity which was to render the close of that century the disgrace of the history of man?" To the gentleman-scholar Jefferson, the sight of "the two most distinguished" nations on earth turning from excellence in "science and civilization" to "robberies and piracies" must have been shocking and reality-altering indeed.[53] To John Adams he writes:

> As for France and England, with all their pre-eminence in science, the one is a den of robbers, and the other of pirates. And if science produces no better fruits than tyranny, murder, rapine and destitution of national morality, I would rather wish our country to be ignorant, honest and estimable as our neighboring savages are.[54]

The vicissitudes of the War of 1812 have convinced him that America can no longer afford the luxury of sending her goods to the "workshops of Europe." Now it is time, proclaims Jefferson, to "place the manufacturer by the side of the agriculturist." And as Jefferson rightly states: "The former question . . . assumes a new form."

> Shall we make our own comforts, or go without them, at the will of a foreign nation? He, therefore, who is now against manufacture, must be for reducing us either to dependence on that foreign nation, or to be clothed in skins, and to live like wild beasts in dens and caverns. I am not one of these; experience has taught me that manufactures are now as necessary to our independence as to our comfort.[55]

Do not be misled; Jefferson is hardly sanguine about this *fait accompli*. After the War of 1812, he writes to his friend and aide William Short that "our enemy has indeed the consolation of Satan on removing our first parents from Paradise: from a peaceable and agricultural nation, he makes us a military and manufacturing one."[56] The realist Jefferson knows that his pastoral vision must be either altered or fatally crushed. Alongside the rolling hills and plowed pastures of Monticello must now stand the industries of Richmond. He hopes that his virtuous citizens, active in the pursuit of public happiness and blessed with the constant economic freedom provided by the availability of land, will not allow the "workshops" and "Canaille" of Europe to develop.

From this discussion of property and pastoralism, some of the implications of Jefferson's political theory begin to manifest themselves. First, there is no natural right to property; such rights are social grants, created to aid men in the pursuit of life, liberty, and happiness. Insofar as economic freedom is necessary to a fully human life, every citizen has to be guaranteed the option of owning a small farm.[57] This instrumentalist view of property is similar to that held by Jean-Jacques Rousseau. While the accumulation of property is not the essence of humanity, a sufficient amount of it is necessary in order to guarantee individual freedom. In his "Discourse on Political Economy" Rousseau calls property a "sacred right," yet he, too, does not consider it a natural right. Society must regulate property so that no "citizen" is rich enough "to buy" another and no "citizen" is so poor as to be forced "to sell" himself. In *The Social Contract* Rousseau proposes legislation that would prevent such "inequalities of fortune; not by building hospitals for the poor, but by securing citizens from becoming poor."[58] Like Paine, Rousseau is writing for a landlocked Europe and consequently has to propose political remedies that are different from Jefferson's grant of fifty acres. But in each thinker the intent is the same: to politically guarantee freedom from an exploitative economic system.

To ensure further economic as well as political freedom, Jefferson advances his principle that the "Earth Belongs to the Living." Once implemented, this principle will guarantee the required periodic alterations in property laws which are so essential to maintaining a society in which all men will have the chance to pursue, if not always to find, happiness. While some scholars have flinched at pushing this argument to its logical conclusion, others have not. In a few passing paragraphs on Jefferson and property, C. B. Macpherson succintly uncovers the function of property in the Jeffersonian scheme:

> With one's own small property one could not be made subservient. And small property was the great guarantee against government tyranny as well as against economic oppression. It was to secure individual liberty, and all the virtues that can flourish only with sturdy independence, that Jefferson wanted America to remain a country of small proprietors.

Pushed to its extreme, the principle becomes much more than merely a right to ownership. Again, Macpherson has captured the crucial point:

> This justification of property rests, in the last analysis, on the right to life at a more than animal level: freedom from coerced labour and arbitrary government are held to be part of what is meant by a fully human life. At the same time this justification is an assertion of the right to the means of labour: the whole point is that by working on his own land or other productive resources a man can be independent and uncoerced.[59]

The second implication is equally cogent, even if it is all too often overlooked. Jefferson is arguing for a right to a particular style of life, a life from which men have a right not to be excluded. This life is associated with the pastoral ideal, which is perhaps best described as a golden mean that reaps the advantages of European art, science, and technology and transplants them to the unsoiled Eden of the New World.[60] Regardless of how feasible this may appear to be, what is important in this image is the explicit rejection of market values in the realization of the good life. Similar claims of economic freedom as a result of the small entrepreneurial farmer have been made by other radical petit-bourgeois theorists in the past, who emphasize the point that bourgeois theory contains its own radical moment. However, the mentality of Jefferson's world view, the ethos that composes and pervades it, brings to the fore a different dimension in his particular brand of radical thought: aesthetic experiences, friendship, community, felicity, leisure—not profitability—are the controlling concerns of this vision.[61]

4

The Nature of Man:
Red, White, and Black

One of the questions you know on which our parties took different sides, was on the improvability of the human mind, in science, in ethics, in government etc. Those who advocated reformation of institutions, pari passu, with the progress of science, maintained that no definite limits could be assigned to that progress. The enemies of reform, on the other hand, denied improvement, and advocated steady adherence to the principles, practices and institutions of our fathers, which they represented as the consummation of wisdom, and akmé of excellence, beyond which the human mind could never advance.[1]

—Jefferson

As with other areas of concern to Jeffersonian scholars, Jefferson presents neither a systematic nor an extended discussion that deals specifically with the theoretical question of the nature of man. He does, fortunately, present his views both on the American Indian and on the American black. From this information it is possible to deduce his concept of man. Stated briefly, Jefferson holds six interrelated postulates concerning human nature: (a) man is largely a creature of his environment; (b) he has an innate moral sense; (c) this moral sense is what makes all men equal; (d) man is naturally sociable; (e) his nature evolves; and (f) evolution can lead to human progress and perfectibility. An extended discussion of Jefferson's writings on, first, the American Indian and then the American slave will bring these properties into sharper focus.'

Because Jefferson was a student and admirer of Francis Bacon, it was natural for him, as an amateur anthropologist, to amass mounds of empirical information on the Indians of North America. Spending much of his youth on the Virginia

53

frontier, he had many opportunities to observe the Indians directly; he even made a detailed study of the different dialects found among the various tribes. Not satisfied solely with his own firsthand observation, Jefferson carefully read the works of others, accepting ones that were based on solid scientific evidence and rejecting ones that were based on myth.[2]

The North American Indian serves Jefferson's political theory much as the noble savage serves Jean-Jacques Rousseau's: each provides a model of men prior to the changes in behavior that are brought about by the forces of modern commercial society. Still, at least one major difference separates Jefferson from Rousseau. Whereas Rousseau's *Second Discourse* is to be read metaphorically, "setting all the facts aside," Jefferson goes to tremendous lengths in attempting to prove the empirical validity of his claims.[3] To him, the American Indian is the closest living specimen to "natural man." Living near the front door of Monticello, these men provided Jefferson's scientific mind with the concrete evidence that he needed so that he could erect a solid democratic political theory.

Toward the end of the year 1780, Jefferson received an extensive list of questions concerning Virginia from the French secretary of legation in the United States, Marquis François de Barbé-Marbois. Fervently, Jefferson set himself to the task at hand. Two reasons account for his intensity: as a scientist, he was committed to the accumulation of knowledge; as a Virginian, he was anxious to refute the common misconceptions held by most Europeans concerning the alleged inferiority of the New World. Of special interest to Jefferson were the writings of the noted naturalist Count de Buffon. The opportunity to challenge Buffon's opinion was a welcomed relief to the past few years that Jefferson had spent in office as governor of Virginia. Even if Jefferson had a difficult time defending his state on the battlefield, he had no similar problems with pen and paper. According to Jefferson, Buffon advanced the following positions: "1. That the animals common both to the old and new world, are smaller in the latter. 2. That those peculiar to the new, are on a smaller scale. 3. That those which have been domesticated in both, have degenerated in America. and 4. That on the whole it exhibits fewer species."[4] One example after another of "brute animals" is presented by Jefferson to challenge Buffon's account. Next, Jefferson focuses on the question of the human inhabitants of the New World.

Buffon notes that the physical stature of the Indians is equal to that of European men, but here any similarities between the two end. The list of points for comparison, and the conclusion drawn from these points, is illustrative of the breadth of Buffon's claim:

> "Although the savage of the new world is about the same height as man in our world, this does not suffice for him to constitute an exception to the general fact that all living nature has become smaller on that continent. The savage is feeble, and has small organs of generation; he has . . . no ardor whatever for his female; although swifter than the European because he is better accustomed to running, he is, on the other hand, less strong in body; he is also less sensitive, and yet more timid and cowardly; he has no vivacity, no activity of mind; the activity of his body is less an exercise, a voluntary motion, than a necessary action caused by want; relieve him of hunger and thirst, and you deprive him of the active principle of all his movements; he will rest stupidly upon his legs or lying down entire days."[5]

From these observations, Buffon concludes:

> "There is no need for seeking further the cause of the isolated mode of life of these savages and their repugnance for society: the most precious spark of the fire of nature has been refused to them; they lack ardor for their females, and consequently have no love for their fellow men: not knowing this strongest and most tender of all affections, their other feelings are also cold and languid; they love their parents and children but little; the most intimate of all ties, the family connection, binds them therefore but loosely together; between family and family there is no tie at all; hence they have no communion, no commonwealth, no state of society."[6]

Both the evidence and the conclusions are disproved by

Jefferson's own firsthand records. Point by point he carefully responds to Buffon.

The Indian is "neither more defective in ardor, nor more impotent with his female." When pressed by necessity, the savage, by Indian standards, is brave. Socialization teaches the Indian that "the point of honor consists in the destruction of an enemy by strategem, and in the preservation of his own person free from injury; . . . while it is education which teaches us to honor force more than finesse." Among the Indians, moreover, "friendships are strong." Yet the bonds of affection naturally recede as they extend beyond the primary group to the secondary and more remote relationships. Because women often attend the men in war and on hunting parties, it becomes difficult to bear children; the use of contraception and abortion is also common practice among Indians. Circumstances, rather than nature, therefore, explain the lower birth rates in North America.[7] The first postulate, (a)—that man is largely a creature of his environment—is now established.

Environmental factors were always critical in Jefferson's reasonings.[8] In a letter in 1785 on the question of the Indians of South America, Jefferson uses differences of environmental circumstances to explain differences in behavior. Don Antonio de Ulloa had advanced the position, similar to Buffon's, that American Indians were inferior to the lower classes of Europe. As always, Jefferson defended the New World. Even though Ulloa's analysis, unlike Buffon's, was based on firsthand observation, by limiting his research to only South American tribes, his work was suspect.

> Don Ulloa's testimony is of the most respectable. He wrote of what he saw. But he saw the Indian of South America only, and that after he had passed through ten generations of slavery. It is very unfair, from this sample, to judge of the natural genius of this race of men: and after supposing that Don Ulloa had not sufficiently calculated the allowance which should be made for this circumstance, we do him no injury in considering the picture he draws of the present Indians of S. America as no picture of what their ancestors were 300 years ago.[9]

The presence of slavery had so scarred the character of the South American Indian that it had become necessary to study their predecessors who were located in the virgin setting of North America. Here, natural man could be observed. Since Jefferson had already completed his research, his position is in contrast to Ulloa's: "The proofs of genius given by the Indians of N. America, place them on a level with Whites in the same uncultivated state."[10] Jefferson boldly claims that "they are formed in mind as well as in body, on the same module with the 'Homo sapiens Europaeus.'" In order to support this contention and to present proof of their genius, he challenges his European readers to furnish "a single passage" of oration, including those of Demosthenes and Cicero, which is "superior to the speech of Logan, a Mingo chief, to Lord Dunmore, when governor of this state."[11]

In *Notes on the State of Virginia* Jefferson proceeds to explore Buffon's contention that the Indians lack society. At first implicitly, and then explicitly in later writings, Jefferson distinguishes between societies with a system of government and those without. The American Indian belongs to the latter category.

"The principles of their society forbidding all compulsion, they are to be led to duty and to enterprize by personal influence and persuasion." A small, closeknit, homogenous community does not need any overt force. Social mores, customs, habits, and public opinion are sufficient mechanisms to regulate society. Jefferson explains that "this practice results from the circumstance of their having never submitted themselves to any laws, any coercive power, any shadow of government. Their only controuls are their manners, and that moral sense of right and wrong, which, like the sense of tasting and feeling, in every man makes a part of his nature."[12] This moral sense, postulate (b), is crucial to understanding Jefferson's politics. Every human being innately possesses this "moral sense," or what on another occasion he calls a "sense of justice"; and this sense, regardless of differences in either reasoning capacity or

57

intellect, allows men to live together peacefully.[13] In a letter
to Peter Carr, written in 1787, these themes of egalitarianism
and innate sociability are again presented.

> He who made us would have been a pitiful bungler if he had
> made the rules of our moral conduct a matter of science. For
> one man of science, there are thousands who are not. What
> would have become of them? Man was destined for society.
> His morality therefore was to be formed to this object. He was
> endowed with a sense of right and wrong merely relative to
> this. This sense is as much a part of his nature as the sense of
> hearing, seeing, feeling; it is the true foundation of morality,
> and not the το χαλον truth, &c., as fanciful writers have
> imagined. The moral sense, or conscience, is as much a part
> of man as his leg or arm.[14]

A year earlier, in one of the most famous and passionate of
Jefferson's private correspondences, the role of the moral
sense is the central concern of the entire letter. Written by
Jefferson to Maria Cosway upon her departure from France
(and Jefferson) to England (and her husband), this letter
takes the form of a dialogue between Jefferson's Head/
Reason and his Heart/Moral Sense. Because of the centrality
of the moral sense to Jefferson's theory and because of the
extraordinary nature of this dialogue-letter, it will be necessary to quote from it at length.

Recognizing the anguish that Jefferson is suffering at the
loss of his friend, the Head initiates the dialogue with a
simple sentence which accurately describes Jefferson's present emotional condition.[15] The Heart affirmatively responds:
"I am indeed the most wretched of all earthly beings.
Overwhelmed with grief, every fibre of my frame distended
beyond it's natural powers to bear, I would willingly meet
whatever catastrophe should leave me no more to feel or to
fear."[16] Rather than to attempt to soothe these fresh wounds
of the senses, the Head seizes the moment in order to
chastise the Heart for always leading both of them into such
painful "scrapes." The Heart points out, however, that it
was the Head that had initiated the contact with the Cos-
ways, as the Head was interested in observing some of the

local architecture. But material things, the Head cautions, are certain, whereas human relationships are far more precarious. The Head then offers some logical, utilitarian advice on how best to conduct one's life:

> In fine, my friend, you must mend your manners. This is not a world to live at random in as you do. To avoid these eternal distresses, to which you are for ever exposing us, you must learn to look forward before you take a step which may interest our peace. Everything in this world is matter of calculation. Advance then with caution, the balance in your hand. Put into one scale the pleasures which any object may offer; but put fairly into the other the pains which are to follow, and see which preponderates. The making an acquaintance is not a matter of indifference. When a new one is proposed to you, view it all round. Consider what advantages it presents, and to what inconveniencies it may expose you. Do not bite at the bait of pleasure till you know there is no hook beneath it. The art of life is the art of avoiding pain: and he is the best pilot who steers clearest of the rocks and shoals with which it is beset. Pleasure is always before us; but misfortune is at our side: while running after that, this arrests us. The most effectual means of being secure against pain is to retire within ourselves, and to suffice for our own happiness. Those, which depend on ourselves, are the only pleasures a wise man will count on: for nothing is ours which another may deprive us of. Hence the inestimable value of intellectual pleasures. . . . Let this be our employ. Leave the bustle and tumult of society to those who have not talents to occupy themselves without them.[17]

The Heart begins its defense by rebalancing the Head's mathematical scale of pain and pleasure. The Heart points out that with the comfort of friends, "grief" can become "almost a luxury." More importantly, the Heart rejects the Head's analysis of the parsimoniousness of life in general. Poetically, Jefferson writes: "But friendship is precious not only in the shade but in the sunshine of life: and thanks to a benevolent arrangement of things, the greater part of life is sunshine." The Heart directly rejects the existence of a solitary soul:

Let the gloomy Monk, sequestered from the world, seek unsocial pleasures in the bottom of his cell! Let the sublimated philosopher grasp visionary happiness while pursuing phantoms dressed in the garb of truth! Their supreme wisdom is supreme folly: and they mistake for happiness the mere absence of pain. Had they ever felt the solid pleasure of one generous spasm of the heart, they would exchange for it all the frigid speculations of their lives, which you have been vaunting in such elevated terms. Believe me then, my friend, that that is a miserable arithmetic which would estimate friendship at nothing, or at less than nothing.[18]

To Jefferson, an existence of "the mind" is not to be confused with a human life: the passions, the Heart, must be an equal partner.

In addition, the whole of life is not a matter of "miserable arithmetic." The Heart lectures the Head that the latter must restrict itself to its proper, natural sphere.

When nature assigned us the same habitation, she gave us over it a divided empire. To you she allotted the field of science, to me that of morals. When the circle is to be squared, or the orbit of a comet to be traced; when the arch of greatest strength, or the solid of least resistance is to be investigated, take you the problem: it is yours: nature has given me no cognisance of it. In like manner in denying to you the feelings of sympathy, of benevolence, of gratitude, of justice, of love, of friendship, she has excluded you from their controul. To these she has adapted the mechanism of the heart. Morals were too essential to the happiness of man to be risked on the incertain combinations of the head. She laid their foundation therefore in sentiment, not in science. That she gave to all, as necessary to all: this to a few only, as sufficing with a few.[19]

Morality is a matter of the senses, not of the intellect; appropriately, nature has given to man a moral sense that enables him, without the aid of calculation, to differentiate right from wrong. Terminating the argument as well as the dialogue, the Heart reminds the Head of two embarrassing instances in their mutual history. On both occasions the Head had prudently counseled personal safety over moral obligations in coming to the aid of strangers who were desperately in need of assistance. Painfully recollecting the circumstances under which the Heart had almost followed the immoral advice of the Head, the Heart castigates the Head: "In short, my friend, as far as my recollection serves me, I do not know that I ever did a good thing on your suggestion, or a dirty one without it."[20] The Head is unable to respond; the Heart is victorious in the debate. But do not misunderstand: The Head is of equal importance to a fully human life. In matters of morality, however, the moral sense, rather than man's reason, is what allows men to live in harmony.

One of the few scholars on Jefferson who argues that the Heart wins the dialogue, Garry Wills, has also pointed out that it is from this perspective that Jefferson writes in the Declaration of Independence that "all men are created equal."[21] As will be seen in the section on slavery, Jefferson does recognize acute differences, some of them innate, between groups of men, but these differences do not extend to man's ability to discern between right and wrong. As Jefferson puts it: "State a moral case to a ploughman and a professor. The former will decide it as well, and often better than the latter, because he has not been led astray by artificial rules."[22] This postulate, (c), will be further established in Jefferson's discussion of slavery.

Along with this moral sense, Jefferson argues for a sense of justice, in addition to the innate sociability of man, postulate (d). Commenting on the foundations for the political theory of Count Destutt de Tracy, Jefferson writes:

> I gather from his other works that he adopts the principle of Hobbes, that justice is founded in contract solely, and does not result from the construction of man. I believe, on the contrary, that it is instinct, and innate, that the moral sense is as much a part of our constitution as that of feeling, seeing, or hearing; as a wise creator must have seen to be necessary in an animal destined to live in society.[23]

As Jefferson conceives of the Universe, its very order and harmony, and the inherent organic make-up of humanity,

61

his conclusions are logical: "Man was created for social intercourse; but social intercourse cannot be maintained without a sense of justice; then man must have been created with a sense of justice."[24] Furthermore, "The practice of morality being necessary for the well-being of society, he has taken care to impress its precepts so indelibly on our hearts that they shall not be effaced by the subtleties of our brain."[25]

The Indians can regulate themselves without the interference of traditional governments because they are moral agents who, in addition to using their moral sense, are receptive to community pressures—for example, loss of esteem, expulsion, and, in extreme cases, execution, carried out by the person who has been damaged. Imperfect as these correctional devices may appear, Jefferson reports that crime among Indian Tribes is low.[26] This is not to say that the Indian communities are leaderless. Chiefs hold "power" through their ability to continually earn the respect of fellow tribesmen, thereby influencing their actions.[27] Furthermore, tribal society suffers no artificial class distinctions, no division between the "wolves and the sheep."[28]

Confronted with the presence of a harmonious community without the presence of a Leviathan, Jefferson rhetorically asks "Whether no law . . . or too much law . . . submits man to the greatest evil?" On the basis of his firsthand observations, he unreservedly concludes that "one who has seen both conditions of existence would pronounce it to be the last: and that the sheep are happier of themselves, than under care of the wolves."[29] He also writes: "I am convinced that those societies (as the Indians) which live without government enjoy in their general mass an infinitely greater degree of happiness than those who live under European governments. Among the former, public opinion is in the place of law, and restrains morals as powerfully as laws ever did any where."[30] This preference for a sort of Kantian anarchism, a community of "lawfulness without laws," is not just a passing whim. Shortly after news of Shays' Rebellion in Massachusetts reached Jefferson, he dispatched a letter to James Madison, in hopes of allaying Madison's fears:

> Those characters wherein fear predominates over hope may apprehend too much from these instances of irregularity. They may conclude too hastily that nature has formed man insusceptible of any other government but that of force, a conclusion not founded in truth, nor experience. Societies exist under three forms sufficiently distinguishable. 1. Without government, as among our Indians. 2. Under governments wherein the will of every one has a just influence, as is the case in England in a slight degree, and in our states in a great one. 3. Under governments of force: as is the case in all other monarchies and in most of the other republics.[31]

Commenting on the forms, he easily characterizes the last type as that of "wolves over sheep." Then, he candidly, yet delicately, raises a question that, he claims, plagues him. "It is a problem, not clear in my mind, that the 1st. condition is not the best." Not content with mere theoretical speculation on the possibility of man's living without coercive government, Jefferson discusses, analyzes, and advocates the desirability of society without either positive law or government. Nevertheless, he readily admits that although the anarchism of the Indian is the optimal social arrangement, it may also be "inconsistent with any great degree of population."[32] As if hinting at the role of decentralization and of community spirit of the ward-republics in his own theory, Jefferson carefully notes how the Indians handle the issue of size:

> Insomuch that were it made a question, whether no law, as among the savage Americans, or too much law, as among the civilized Europeans, submits man to the greatest evil, one who has seen both conditions of existence would pronounce it to be the last: and that the sheep are happier of themselves, than under care of the wolves. It will be said, that great societies cannot exist without government. The Savages therefore break them into small ones.[33]

Jefferson's writings about the American Indian demonstrate that he rejects the "liberal," atomistic interpretation of society; and his understanding of Indian society does not view it as the expression of an extreme individualism, logically terminating in the anarchism of Proudhon. Rather, man is a social being. Unlike Hobbes, Locke, and even Rousseau, who all begin with arguments that assume an original sovereignty over oneself, Jefferson bases his theory on sociability, not on individuality. He rejects the notion of a contract with oneself: "To ourselves, in strict language, we can owe no duties, obligation requiring also two parties. Self-love, therefore, is no part of morality."[34] The Indians need few positive laws, because shared ideals, customs, and pasts can bind these untainted men together with bonds of affection and friendship. Coercion, under these circumstances, would be superfluous. And since man as an individual is naturally both social and moral, there is, to Jefferson's mind, no reason for him, as a member of a community, to behave in a contrary manner. To Madison he writes:

> I know but one code of morality for men whether acting singly or collectively. He who says I will be a rogue when I act in company with a hundred others but an honest man when I act alone, will be believed in the former assertion, but not in the latter. I would say with the poet, *"hic niger est, hunc tu Romane cavato."* If the morality of one man produces a just line of conduct in him, acting individually, why should not the morality of 100 men produce a just line of conduct in them, acting together?[35]

The American Indian, then, gives Jefferson a model of man prior to and removed from the forces of emerging commercial society. Whereas political theorists from Hobbes to Madison had based their political systems on a market model of man and consequently saw the need for a strong coercive power to hold these possessive individualists at bay, Jefferson witnesses the possibilities of having domestic tranquility without the aid of government.[36] Thus far, Jefferson's views on the nature of men have been presented principally through his writings on the American Indians, among whom there were degrees of development, of evolution, as is apparent in a letter from Jefferson to William Ludlow. This letter, in language that sounds as if it has been taken from Hegel's *Phenomenology of Mind*, establishes the last two postulates, (e) and (f), to Jefferson's concept of man:

> Let a philosophic observer commence a journey from the savages of the Rocky Mountains, eastwardly towards our seacoast. These he would observe in the earliest stage of association living under no law but that of nature, subsisting and covering themselves with the flesh and skins of wild beasts. He would next find those on our frontiers in the pastoral state, raising domestic animals to supply the defects of hunting. Then succeed our own semi-barbarous citizens, the pioneers of the advance of civilization, and so on in his progress he would meet the gradual shades of improving man until he would reach his, as yet, most improved state in our seaport towns. This, in fact, is equivalent to a survey, in time, of the progress of man from the infancy of creation to the present day. I am eighty-one years of age, born where I now live, in the first range of mountains in the interior of our country. And I have observed this march of civilization advancing from the seacoast, passing over us like a cloud of light, increasing our knowledge and improving our condition, insomuch as that we are at this time more advanced in civilization here than the seaports were when I was a boy. And where this progress will stop no one can say. Barbarism has, in the meantime, been receding before the steady step of amelioration; and will in time, I trust, disappear from the earth.[37]

Clearly, Jefferson recognizes the evolving, developmental quality of men. But unlike the Great Chain of Being theorists, Jefferson's ontology held no absolute *telos*.[38] Within the confines of his evolutionary scheme, the American slave held the lowest position, supporting on his back both the Indian and his white master. A discussion of Jefferson and slavery can be postponed no longer.

The most formidable aspects in the political theory of Thomas Jefferson to come to terms with are his views on black Americans and slavery. The problem lies not so much in attempting to offer an explanation or an apology or a rationalization of his ownership of scores of slaves as in presenting in a coherent manner his complex, often ambivalent, and usually parochial perspectives on the issue.[39] Still, on at least three points concerning slavery, Jefferson was clear: first, although they are "probably" inferior in talents to other members of the human family, blacks are still "equal" in that they, too, possess a moral sense; second, slavery is morally wrong; and third, with regard to the issue of slavery, theory and practice must be kept separate.

While drafting the Declaration of Independence, Jefferson incorporated a lengthy paragraph addressing the immoral conduct of the king in aiding the perpetuation of the slave trade. In the list of indictments against the monarch, he writes:

> He has waged cruel war against human nature itself, violating it's most sacred rights of life and liberty in the persons of a distant people who never offended him, captivating & carrying them into slavery in another hemisphere or to incur miserable death in their transportation thither. This piratical warfare, the opprobrium of *infidel* powers, is the warfare of the *Christian* king of Great Britain, determined to keep open a market where *Men* should be bought & sold, he has prostituted his negative for suppressing every legislative attempt to prohibit or to restrain this execrable commerce.[40]

Although this list was expunged from the final, official copy of the Declaration of Independence, Jefferson was anxious that posterity should know precisely what he had written in the original draft. Several copies, personally handwritten by Jefferson, were circulated by him; and in his *Autobiography*, he again copied the complete draft of the Declaration, lest it become lost.

Angry and upset at the actions of his fellow revolutionaries, Jefferson recognized the political reality of the situation. The majority of Americans were unwilling to freely divest themselves of their slave assets.[41] Therefore, at this point in history, practicality must rule. Rather than push the issue of slavery, thus antagonizing the Southern States and losing the desperately needed unanimous support for independence, Jefferson reluctantly acquiesced. This was but the first of many incidents in which Jefferson felt that pragmatic considerations, and the hopes of emancipation in the long run, outweighed the immediate principle.

Even while he was writing the Declaration of Independence, Jefferson was drafting model constitutions for his state of Virginia. In these models, slavery is expressly prohibited.[42] In later models, the prohibition is maintained, with the proviso that the newly freed slaves must leave the state within one year.[43] Refusing Jefferson's unsolicited advice, the Virginia Constitutional Convention reaffirmed the status of slavery. Once more, neither Jefferson nor his allies felt inclined to push the point. He explained his actions in this way: "The moment of doing it with success was not yet arrived, and . . . an unsuccessful effort, as too often happens, would only rivet still closer the chains of bondage, and retard the moment of delivery to this oppressed description of men."[44] Similarly, as president of the United States, he was careful, above all, to do no harm to the cause of freedom. When asked to tacitly endorse an antislavery pamphlet entitled "A Tragical Poem on the Oppression of the Human Species," he refused, saying, "I have most carefully avoided every public act or manifestation on that subject. Should an occasion ever occur in which I can interpose with decisive effect, I shall certainly know & do my duty with promptitude & zeal. But in the meantime It would only be disarming myself of influence to be taking small means."[45]

His continued ownership of slaves he also explained, but never justified, on prudential grounds. As a citizen of the state of Virginia, Jefferson was bound by its laws; and its laws regarding slavery were strict. If any slaveholder wished to free his slaves, he had to provide for them to be transported out of Virginia; if he failed to do so, any other Virginian could reenslave them. Obviously, merely providing them with passage beyond the boundaries of the state was hardly enough to ensure manumission. Physical freedom required that they be transported out of Virginia and that they be provided with ample funds so that the slaves could begin to secure their own livelihood. All such action, however, fails to take into account the psychological scars that have crippled the slaves. Only the hardiest of black men could survive in eighteenth-century America as a citizen. In an 1814 letter to James Madison's secretary, Edward Coles, Jefferson expresses this position. Employing his familiar rhetorical device of questions and answers, he asks, "Are you right in abandoning this property?" and answers:

> I think not. My opinion has ever been that, until more can be done for them, we should endeavor, with those whom fortune has thrown on our hands, to feed and clothe them well, protect them from all ill usage, require such reasonable labor only as is performed voluntarily by freemen, & be led by no repugnancies to abdicate them, and our duties to them. The laws do not permit us to turn them loose, if that were for their good: and to commute them for other property is to commit them to those whose usage of them we cannot control.[46]

Although he shows a concern for the plight of blacks, Jefferson's wording of the question, which equates men with property, shows how he was never really able to transcend his own cultural heritage. Prior to the letter to Coles, Jefferson had already equated his own slaves with property. They were assets that he said he would eventually part with—but only after they had produced enough wealth to allow him to become solvent. Failing to extricate himself from debt during his lifetime, it was only at his death that Jefferson manumitted a few slaves. But even here, he claims to be "governed solely by views to their happiness."[47] Nevertheless, it shows to what extent the institution of slavery entraps the master as well as the slave.

This parochialism is carried over to Jefferson's theoretical views on blacks, where he often fails to adopt the same rigorously scientific stance that he finds useful in his defense of Indians against the charges of Don Ulloa, discussed above.[48] Whereas Jefferson refuses to accept generalizations that have been drawn from one culture and applied to an entire race, as was done in Ulloa's study, he is more amenable to accepting conclusions concerning the inferiority of blacks.

In *Notes on the State of Virginia* he cautiously observes that "the opinion, that they are inferior in the faculties of reason and imagination, must be hazarded with great diffidence. To justify a general conclusion, requires many obervations." After recognizing the need for further research, he nevertheless writes that "I advance it therefore as a suspicion only, that the blacks . . . are inferior to the whites in the endowments both of body and mind."[49] His own prejudices come out while discussing the differences between blacks, Indians, and whites. Rather than chronicle all the points of inferiority that Jefferson observes, an example can be illustrative. Beginning with the obvious, Jefferson notes the difference in pigmentation:

> The first difference which strikes us is that of colour. Whether the black of the negro resides in the reticular membrane between the skin and scarf-skin, or in the scarf-skin itself; whether it proceeds from the colour of the blood, the colour of the bile, or from that of some other secretion, the difference is fixed in nature, and is as real as if its seat and cause were better known to us. And is this difference of no importance? Is it not the foundation of a greater or less share of beauty in the two races? Are not the fine mixtures of red and white, the expressions of every passion by greater or less suffusions of colour in the one, preferable to that eternal monotony, which reigns in the countenances, that immoveable veil of black which covers all the emotions of the other race? Add to these, flowing hair, a more elegant symmetry of form, their own judgment in favour of the whites, declared by their preference of them, as uniformly as is the preference of the Oran-ootan for the black women over those of his own species. The circumstance of superior beauty, is thought worthy attention in the propagation of our horses, dogs, and other domestic animals; why not in that of man?[50]

While he equates the Indian and the European in terms of beauty and while he readily acknowledges the inferiority of blacks, Jefferson always believes in human development and education. Consequently, he holds out the hypothesis that in time, cultivated in a friendly society, blacks can become fully equal to the other Americans. In 1785 he writes to the Marquis de Chastellux: "I believe the Indian then to be in body and mind equal to the whiteman. I have supposed the blackman, in his present state, might not be so. But it would be hazardous to affirm that, equally cultivated for a few generations, he would not become so."[51]

Jefferson continued throughout his life to look for evidence to challenge his own views on the racial inferiority of blacks. While he was in France, he translated and took careful notes on Condorcet's views of slavery.[52] Back in the United States, he wrote to that philosophe, informing him of the progress of a black American mathematician who was employed in the planning of the new capital, had recently written an almanac, and was "a very worthy & respectable member of society." Not convinced by an isolated example, Jefferson tells Condorcet that he (Jefferson) will "be delighted to see these instances of moral eminence so multiplied as to prove that the want of talents observed in them is merely the effect of their degraded condition, and not proceeding from any difference in the structure of the parts on which intellect depends."[53] Almost twenty years later, he was still looking for evidence that would be supportive of Condorcet. Henri Grégoire sent to Jefferson *Literature of Negroes*, which the latter graciously thanked him for, claiming "that no person living wishes more sincerely than I do, to see a complete refutation of doubts I have myself entertained and expressed on the grade of understanding allotted to them by nature." The nature of Jefferson's own views, he explains to Grégoire, is "the result of personal observation on the limited sphere of my own State, where the opportunities for the development of their [the blacks'] genius were not favorable, and those of exercising it still less so."[54]

The question then arises: Why does Jefferson ardently defend the innate abilities and capacities of the North American Indian, while, at best, he reluctantly accepts any evidence supporting the talents of blacks? Undoubtedly, sheer prejudice supplies part of the response. He was surrounded by two contrasting models of man: noble savages and ignorant slaves. In theory, he can speculate on the potential mental equality of all men, but direct exposure seems to belie that possibility. The fact that the Indians were native Americans, whereas the slaves were "imports," is also crucial to understanding Jefferson. He must have felt honor-bound to prove that there is nothing inferior about either the New World or its original inhabitants. He alleges that America grows better vegetation, supports heartier animals, and nurtures good, cultured men. If the claim could have been sustained that environmental factors have caused the Indian to be inferior, the corollary allegation that it might have a similar debilitating effect on Europeans would thereby gain credence. For this, Jefferson will not stand. Indeed, he wants to prove that, if anything, the New World provides mankind with the unique opportunity of starting anew on a fresh, virgin setting, removed from the rot of Europe.

In many ways, this debate on Jefferson's views about the attributes of black Americans is misdirected, because—physical and mental abilities aside—simply as men, they have to be considered equal, postulate (c) in the one sense that matters —namely, they are human, and therefore they, too, possess the moral sense. In *Notes on the State of Virginia* Jefferson confronts the problem of thefts committed by black slaves. His response is interesting: he argues that it is not because they lack a moral sense that slaves steal but, rather, because they are not bound to any social arrangement, since reciprocity is absent·

> Whether further observation will or will not verify the conjecture, that nature has been less bountiful to them in the endowments of the head, I believe that in those of the heart [i.e., moral sense] she will be found to have done them justice. That disposition to theft with which they have been branded, must be ascribed to their situation, and no depravity of the moral sense. The man, in whose f

laws of property exist, probably feels himself less bound to respect those made in favour of others. When arguing for ourselves, we lay it down as a fundamental, that laws, to be just, must give a reciprocation of right: that, without this, they are mere arbitrary rules of conduct, founded in force, and not in conscience: and it is a problem which I give to the master to solve, whether the religious precepts against the violation of property were not framed for him as well as his slave? And whether the slave may not as justifiably take a little from one, who has taken all from him, as he may slay one who would slay him? That a change in the relations in which a man is placed should change his ideas of moral right and wrong, is neither new, nor peculiar to the colour of the blacks. . . . Notwithstanding these considerations which must weaken their respect for the laws of property, we find among them numerous instances of the most rigid integrity, and as many as among their better instructed masters, of benevolence, gratitude, and unshaken fidelity.[55]

Consequently, blacks must also be allowed to enjoy the same rights as all men. Remembering the exalted position of Newton as part of the trinity in Jefferson's own belief system, his egalitarian comments to Grégoire take on symbolic importance: "Whatever be their degree of talent it is no measure of their rights. Because Sir Isaac Newton was superior to others in understanding, he was not therefore lord of the person or property of others."[56] Since blacks and whites are members of "the same human family," it is "self-evident" to Jefferson that slavery is an abomination which must be brought to an end, willingly or unwillingly.

In the final analysis, he believes that economics, education, and Providence will terminate slavery. In 1805 he doubts "any early provision for the extinguishment of slavery among us." The morality of the issue, he writes, is not as clear-cut to the community as it is to himself. "There are many virtuous men who would make any sacrifices to affect it, many equally virtuous who persuade themselves either that the thing is not wrong, or that it cannot be remedied, and very many with whom interest is morality." He thinks that changes in the economic make-up of the

Southern States since the turn of the century are becoming
increasingly advantageous to the eventual emancipation of
the slaves. "But interest," writes Jefferson, "is really going
over to the side of morality. The value of the slavery is
everyday lessening; his burden on his master daily increasing."[57] In terms of the commercial tobacco trade, slaves were
rapidly becoming unprofitable; and yet, Jefferson did not
foresee the rise of the cotton South. Economic realities
would not play as large a role as quickly as he prophesied.

A certain order, harmony, and justice pervade Jefferson's
universe. This leads him to confront the apocalyptic conclusion that it will be but a matter of time until divine intervention will strike on behalf of the slave. In 1821, at the age of
seventy-seven, Jefferson writes in his *Autobiography:* "Nothing is more certainly written in the book of fate than that
these people are to be free."[58] Among the most sublime and
passionate prose ever penned by the prolific Jefferson is that
on the inhuman plight of the slave:

> Indeed I tremble for my country when I reflect that God is
> just: that his justice cannot sleep for ever: that considering
> numbers, nature and natural means only, a revolution of the
> wheel of fortune, an exchange of situation, is among possible
> events: that it may become probable by supernatural inter-
> ference! The Almighty has no attribute which can take sides
> with us in such a contest.[59]

Shortly thereafter he writes:

> But we must await with patience the workings of an overrul-
> ing providence, and hope that that is preparing the deliv-
> erance of these our suffering brethren. When the measure of
> their tears shall be full, when their groans shall have involved
> heaven itself in darkness, doubtless a god of justice will
> awaken to their distress, and by diffusing light and liberality
> among their oppressors, or at length by his exterminating
> thunder, manifest his attention to the things of this world,
> and that they are not left to the guidance of a blind fatality.[60]

If either God or Mammon should fail to remedy th\~ evil,
education and the ensuing generation will do so: '

them I look, to the rising generation, and not to the one now in power for these great reformations."[61] He senses that change is in the air: "The spirit of the master is abating, that of the slave rising from the dust, his condition mollifying, the way I hope preparing, under the auspices of heaven, for a total emancipation, and that this is disposed, in the order of events, to be with the consent of the masters, rather than by their extirpation."[62] His unflinching faith in the power and importance of education never abandoned Jefferson. Until his death, he willingly bequeathed all social problems to the next generation: as man develops and becomes more enlightened, all shackles on his progress will wither away.

Jefferson is positive that slavery will eventually die out. He is equally sure that due to "deep rooted prejudices entertained by the whites . . . [and] ten thousand recollections, by the blacks, of injuries they have sustained," the two races can never live together peacefully.[63] So in addition to being freed and educated, the slaves were to be colonized, preferably in Africa.[64] While the American Indian can be assimilated into the white New World, the American slave cannot be.

His views on the American slave and the American Indian having been considered, it is now possible to summarize Jefferson's concept of man. During the late eighteenth century, the idea of "perfectibility" was gaining wide acceptance as the theory of the Great Chain of Being was receding. Writing to Bishop James Madison, Jefferson comments favorably on the proposition made by William Godwin, Adam Weishaupt, Richard Price, and Joseph Priestley, who thought that man "may in time be rendered so perfect that he will be able to govern himself in every circumstance so as to injure none, to do all the good he can, to leave government no occasion to exercise their power over him, & of course to render political government useless."[65] Europe has grown to such proportions as to preclude this style of community, but the Indian experience of creating small pockets of communities within larger tribes sets the tone for

Jefferson's small ward-republics. In several letters to John Adams, the question of perfectibility again arises. Jefferson responds that this has always been a point of contention between the two men because Jefferson believes in the "improvability of the human mind," whereas Adams does not.[66] To Jefferson, man is not static, fixed. He develops, evolves. Although man possesses a moral sense, this, as with all human faculties, also evolves.[67]

Jefferson, therefore, simultaneously holds several postulates on human nature: (a) man is largely a creature of his environment; (b) he has an innate moral sense; (c) this moral sense is what makes all men equal; (d) man is naturally sociable; (e) his nature evolves; and (f) evolution can lead to human progress and perfectibility. If one is aware that man actively participates in the creation of his environment and that his environment can have either an impeding (as in an urban center) or an enhancing (as in a bucolic setting) effect on his development, then the quality of the social milieu is critical to the human pursuit of life, liberty, and happiness— a happiness and a life, moreover, that is distinctly non-market in its ethos. It is also essential for man's individual as well as his collective well-being that the society, its laws, and its institutions keep pace with human progress. If they do not, this, too, may have a retarding, rather than an enriching, impact on man. In the spirit of his principle that the earth belongs to the living, Jefferson emphasizes this point:

> But I know also, that laws and institutions must go hand in hand with the progress of the human mind. As that becomes more developed, more enlightened, as new discoveries are made, new truths disclosed, and manners and opinions change with the change of circumstances, institutions must advance also, and keep pace with the times. We might as well require a man to wear still the coat which fitted him when a boy, as civilized society to remain ever under the regimen of their barbarous ancestors.[68]

With Jefferson's views on economics and man established, it is appropriate to turn to his position on government.

75

5
Jeffersonian Government: Public and Private Happiness

Divide the counties into wards of such size as that every citizen can attend, when called on, and act in person. Ascribe to them the government of their wards in all things relating to themselves exclusively . . . and by making every citizen an acting member of the government, and in the offices nearest and most interesting to him, will attach him by his strongest feelings to the independence of his country, and its republican constitution. . . . These wards, called townships in New England, are the vital principle of their governments, and have proved themselves the wisest invention ever devised by the wit of man for the perfect exercise of self-government, and for its preservation.[1]

—Jefferson

As was commonplace for an eighteenth-century gentleman interested in politics, Jefferson expended considerable time and effort in writing about government. He found the roles of social critic and constitutional architect to be much to his liking. In commenting on the United States Constitution of 1787, his response was usually cool, although on a few occasions he displayed open hostility to the draft. He told several friends he hoped that it would not be ratified. Even with the knowledge of James Madison's personal investment in the creation of the Constitution, Jefferson suggested to Madison that even though the document was an interesting first effort, he and his compatriots ought to try again.[2] Written in isolation from Paris, Jefferson's advice was ignored. The Constitution, with the promise of a Bill of Rights, for which Jefferson lobbied, was approved and implemented. Architectonically, Jefferson constructed several model constitutions for the state of Virginia. In June and July of 1776, while composing the Declaration of Independence,

Jefferson found it relaxing to spend time drafting constitutions for his home state, which would soon be holding its own constitutional convention. In reading these papers, the central characteristics of Jefferson's ideal for good government become evident. In an editorial note to Jefferson's constitutions, Julian Boyd presents the following as the leading principles in Jefferson's theory:

> . . . the people as the source of authority; the protection of "public liberty" and of individual rights against authoritarian control; the widening of suffrage and an equalization of the distribution of representation in the legislative branch; the use of unappropriated lands for the establishment of a society of independent farmers who would hold their lands "in full and absolute dominion of no superior whatever"; the just and equitable treatment of the Indians; the use of the western lands so as to remove friction with neighboring states and promote the cause of nationality; the encouragement of immigration and the lowering of barriers to naturalization; the elevation of the civil over the military authority; the abolition of privilege and prerogative; and so on.[3]

Though Boyd locates many important issues in Jefferson's constitutions, it is suffrage, Jefferson argues, that is the true foundation of popular government.

In his letter to Samuel Kercheval, dated 12 July 1816, Jefferson remarks "that a government is republican in proportion as every member composing it has his equal voice in the direction of its concerns." With this, the primary criterion of "republicanism" in hand, it is not surprising that Jefferson should ask, and then rhetorically answer, the obvious question: "Where then is our republicanism to be found? Not in our constitution certainly, but merely in the spirit of our people." Jefferson tells Kercheval: "The true foundation of republican government is the equal right of every citizen, in his person and property, and in their management." He concludes: "Try by this, as a tally, every provision of our constitution, and see if it hangs directly on the will of the people. Reduce your legislature to a convenient number for full, but orderly discussion. Let every man who fights or pays, exercise his just and equal right in their election.''[4] On this basis, Jefferson unequivocally feels that the Virginia Constitution does not "hang directly on the will of the people''; consequently, in this private letter, Jefferson urges Kercheval to strive for its replacement with a more democratic document.

This position of Jefferson's in favor of universal white-manhood suffrage, along with equal representation, remained with him throughout his life. Given the crucial nature of this issue to any political theory that claims to be democratic, I will present a chronological account of Jefferson's views on suffrage.

In his *Notes on the State of Virginia* Jefferson explains that the original Virginia Constitution was framed by men, including himself, who were "unexperienced in the science of government.'' As a result, "the majority of men in the State, who pay and fight for its support, are unrepresented in the legislature, the roll of the freeholders entitled to vote not including generally the half of those on the roll of the militia, or of the taxgatherers.''[5] In spite of the fact that the "Founding Fathers'' of Virginia considered their state to be a republic, the claim could no longer stand up to the Jeffersonian standards of 1781. Two score and two years later, Jefferson was still arguing that most of the state governments were undemocratic in that they restricted the right to vote: "And add, also, that one half of our brethren who fight and pay taxes, are excluded, like Helots, from the rights of representation, as if society were instituted for the soil and not for the men inhabiting it; or one half of these could dispose of the rights and the will of the other half, without their consent.''[6]

In addition to his contention about the limitation on suffrage, Jefferson always argues against the inequality of representation given the apportionment standards employed in Virginia. Between some counties, the ratio of voting weights was seventeen to one; this, he claimed, could not be tolerated in republican governments.[7]

To avoid any misunderstanding, it must be pointed out

that in an early draft of a proposed constitution for Virginia, Jefferson, on the surface, appears to provide for a rather limited suffrage because voting is to be restricted to "All male persons of full age & sane mind having a freehold estate in (¼ of an acre) of land in any town, or in (25) acres of land in the country, & all persons resident in the colony who shall have paid scot & lot to government the last (two years)." However, this passage is elucidated later in the same document where Jefferson has a curious paragraph under the general heading "Rights Private and Public." There he writes: "Every person of full age neither owning nor having owned (50) acres of land, shall be entitled to an appropriation of (50) acres or to so much as shall make up what he owns or has owned (50) acres in full and absolute dominion, and no other person shall be capable of taking an appropriation."[8] As prior chapters demonstrate, Jefferson wants all males to own land; and apparently, he wants them to own at least fifty acres. In addition to economic freedom, the right to own property will simultaneously give every male the vote, and also political freedom. It must be concluded, then, that from the start of his public life, Jefferson was an unwavering advocate of universal suffrage for white males.

In another hypothetical constitution, dated 1783, Jefferson directly extended the vote to "All free male citizens of full age and sane mind, who for one year before shall have been resident in the county, or shall through the whole of that time have possessed therein real property of the value of ——— or shall have for the same time have been enrolled in the militia."[9] Finally, returning to the Kercheval letter of 1816, we find Jefferson still advocating universal suffrage as he specifically lists "General Suffrage" as the first in a series of reform amendments that he recommends to the young Virginia as being necessary for its democratization.[10]

A final note on suffrage: Although Jefferson grasped the centrality of the vote for a fully human, democratic life, he was unwilling to make suffrage genuinely universal by extending it beyond white males. On at least two occasions,

Jefferson explicitly argued for the disenfra
women, in order to "protect" them from the
affairs.[11] And the possibility of giving th
Americans appears never to have surfaced in his

General suffrage, equal representation, separation of
powers, and popular sovereignty are incorporated in all of
Jefferson's model constitutions. Yet, in his last efforts at
constitution building, after a lifetime of public service, he
feels a growing urgency to create a public space where all
citizens can actively participate in governmental affairs, and
thereby ensure their freedom and their pursuit of public
happiness. Indeed, among the Founding Fathers, Jefferson
alone wishes to institutionalize general education, participatory democracy, and permanent revolution through the
establishment of ward-republics.

The infatuation with ward-republics appears in several
pieces of Jefferson's private correspondences. In a letter to
Governor Tyler, dated 26 May 1810, Jefferson shuns Tyler's
suggestion that he return to the Virginia legislature. Preferring the tranquility of Monticello and the power of the pen,
Jefferson tells the governor that he is engaged in "two great
measures at heart without which no republic can maintain
itself"—namely, general education and the creation of
wards. In this letter he explains how the subdivision of the
"general" republic into "little republics" would be a positive boon if rapid, mass mobilization should ever be required
against either a foreign or a domestic threat. Jefferson
describes the process thus:

> General orders are given out from a center to the foreman of
> every hundred, as to the sergeants of an army, and the whole
> nation is thrown into energetic action, in the same direction
> in one instant and as one man. . . . Could I once see this I
> should consider it as the dawn of salvation of the republic,
> and say with old Simeon, *"nunc dimittas Domine."*[12]

In 1816 Jefferson writes two additional letters that contain
more-extensive discussions of the rationale behind the ward-
republics: the first letter is to Joseph Cabell; the second, to
Samuel Kercheval. To Cabell, Jefferson introduces the topic

by suggesting that public education should be locally controlled; he points out that the division of the county into wards could be expedited if the division were made coterminous with the already existing "militia captaincies." In addition to providing a base for public education, these wards would become the keystone in Jefferson's entire political process. "The way to have a good and safe government," advises Jefferson, "is not to trust it all to one, but to divide it among the many, distributing to everyone exactly the functions he is competent to." He further supplements his ward-republics, therefore, with a four-tiered, pyramidal structure of government: the national government forms the peak and is "entrusted with the defense of the nation, and its foreign and federal relations"; the next level, consisting of the state governments, is concerned with "the civil rights, laws, police and administration of what concerns the state generally"; the third quarter confronts "the local concerns of the counties"; and the ward-republics, which compose the base, "direct the interests within itself."[13] In the Kercheval letter, the democratic Jefferson argues that in the ward-republics, as in William Godwin's parishes, every official position, including judges, juries, and sheriffs, should be elective; he did not find convincing the popular argument that judicial questions should be the exclusive reserve of those who are trained and educated in the law.[14] Each division of the pyramid functions as a republic; each is dependent on the next subordinate level for its authority and guidance.

> The elementary republics of the wards, the county republics, the state republics, and the republic of the Union, would form a graduation of authorities, standing each on the basis of law, holding everyone its delegated share of powers, and constituting truly a system of fundamental balances and checks for the government. Where every man is a sharer in the direction of his ward-republic, or of some of the higher ones, and feels that he is a participator in the government of affairs, not merely at an election one day in the year, but every day; when there shall not be a man in the state who will

> not be a member of some one of its councils, great or small, he will let the heart be torn out of his body sooner than his power be wrested from him by a Caesar or a Bonaparte.[15]

Division and subdivision, "until it ends in the administration of everyman's farm by himself," then, is the mechanism by which political freedom is guaranteed.[16] Mere periodic elections are not enough for a democratic theory: "every day" a man must be a "participator in the government of affairs." And in the upper levels, the representatives are to be held accountable by short terms of office.[17]

In Jefferson's schema, which is patterned both on the New England townships that he admiringly characterized as "the wisest invention ever devised by the wit of man" and on the American Indians' tribal councils, he hoped to make "every citizen an acting member of government." The ward-republics will provide the proper mixture whereby "the whole is cemented by giving to every citizen, personally, a part in the administration of the public affairs." Obviously, to Jefferson, politics is not the activity of a noble few, but rather a noble activity in which every member of society will be involved, in order to earn the title "citizen." Certainly, with his advocacy of requiring each citizen to give his vote viva voce and with his insistence on dividing "the counties into wards of such size that every citizen can attend . . . and act in person," Jefferson's views are in harmony with the ancient Greek conceptions of politics and citizenship.[18]

The ward-republics, then, are to fulfill a fourfold function: (1) to check the petty tyrants at home; (2) to maintain the revolutionary spirit of 1776; (3) to provide a base for general education; and (4) to ensure a space in which the citizens can become proficient in the art of politics.[19] This last function, which is often overlooked in Jefferson, has two distinct but complementary parts. The first, which has already been discussed, deals specifically with the creation of a public space for the daily activity of local politics. The second, elaborated below, concerns Jefferson's desire to provide for every generation the opportunity to create its own political community.

In the entire galaxy of secondary studies of Jefferson's political philosophy, only Hannah Arendt firmly grasps the importance of both aspects of the fourth function of the ward-republic in Jefferson's governmental system:

> [Jefferson] knew, however dimly, that the Revolution, while it had given freedom to the people, had failed to provide a space where this freedom could be exercised. Only the representatives of the people, not the people themselves, had an opportunity to engage in those activities of "expressing, discussing and deciding" which in a positive sense are the activities of freedom.
>
> . . . .
>
> On the American scene, no one has perceived this seemingly inevitable flaw in the structure of the republic with greater clarity and more passionate preoccupation than Jefferson. His occasional, and sometimes violent, antagonism against the Constitution . . . was motivated by a feeling of outrage about the injustice that only his generation should have it in their power "to begin the world over again."[20]

Jefferson never faltered in his belief that "no society can make a perpetual constitution, or even a perpetual law. The earth always belongs to the living generation."[21] The "fresh start" that he and his contemporaries had been given in the American experience must somehow be passed on to each succeeding generation. Each generation must be allowed to begin anew. Each must redefine its goals and ideals; all must recommit themselves to each other. It is essential to a democratic community that each generation be able to "depute representatives to a convention, and to make the constitution what they think will be the best for them."[22] Jefferson recognizes the necessity of recreating the constitutional congresses and conventions of the 1770s and 1780s. A mere reshuffling of the government will not do. Using the mechanism of the small ward-republics, Jefferson argues that all citizens could thereby be incorporated into the political processes of legislation and governance:

> That majority, then, has a right to depute representatives to a convention, and to make the constitution what they think

will be the best for themselves. But how collect their voice? This is the real difficulty. If invited by private authority, or county or district meetings, these divisions are so large that few will attend; and their voice will be imperfectly, or falsely pronounced. Here, then, would be one of the advantages of the ward divisions I have proposed. The mayor of every ward, on a question like the present, would call his ward together, take the simple yea or nay of its members, convey these to the county court, who would hand on those of all its wards to the proper general authority; and the voice of the whole people would be thus fairly, fully, and peaceably expressed, discussed, and decided by the common reason of the society.

Through ward-republics, "the voice of the whole people would be thus fairly, fully, and peaceably expressed, discussed, and decided by the common reason of the society." This participation alone, says Jefferson, would make a "true democracy."[23] Anything short of this process allows for the rule of the dead from beyond the grave.

The creation of a public space is intimately linked with the maintenance of a spirit of revolution in the society at large. Having been in the foreground of several revolutions, Jefferson appears to have found the experiences refreshing. His letters on revolution convey a sense of catharsis, of cleansing, of providing an opportunity to begin again. In 1787 Jefferson produced two of his more famous quotations on this topic. Eager to quiet James Madison over the past rebellion in Massachusetts, he writes:

> I hold it that a little rebellion now and then is a good thing, and as necessary in the political world as storms in the physical. Unsuccessful rebellions indeed generally establish the incroachments on the rights of the people which have produced them. An observation of this truth should render honest republican governors so mild in their punishment of rebellions, as not to discourage them too much. It is a medicine necessary for the sound health of government.[24]

And to William Smith, once more on Shays' Rebellion, Jefferson explains,

God forbid we should ever be 20. years without such a rebellion. . . . We have had 13. states independent 11. years. There has been one rebellion. That comes to one rebellion in a century and a half for each state. What country before ever existed a century and half without a rebellion? And what country can preserve it's liberties if their rulers are not warned from time to time that their people preserve the spirit of resistance? Let them take arms. The remedy is to set them right as to facts, pardon and pacify them. What signify a few lives lost in a century or two? The tree of liberty must be refreshed from time to time with the blood of patriots and tyrants. It is it's natural manure.[25]

Even as an elder statesman, Jefferson's fervently optimistic belief in revolution remains intact. The need for permanent revolution is apparent in his 4 September 1823 letter to John Adams, in which Jefferson notes that "the generation which commences a revolution can rarely compleat it." Hence, it is necessary to keep the spirit of change alive. Self-government is a *sine qua non* to a fully human life. To achieve and maintain this style of life may be costly, as Jefferson shows: "To attain all this however rivers of blood must yet flow, and years of desolation pass over. Yet the object is worth rivers of blood, and years of desolation for what inheritance so valuable can man leave to his posterity."[26] Hannah Arendt also understands the revolutionary nature of Jefferson's ward-republics. Indeed, she accurately compares them to the "Parisian Commune . . . *soviets* and *Räte.*" With equal accuracy she notes that Jefferson's proposals were completely ignored by "statesmen, historians, political theorists, and, most importantly, by the revolutionary tradition itself . . . [because] they failed to understand to what an extent the council system confronted them with an entirely new form of government, with a new public space for freedom which was constituted and organized during the course of the revolution itself."[27]

Once the ward-republics are understood within the context of the overall Jeffersonian system, other aspects of his theory become more comprehensible. For instance, his advocacy of a constitutional convention every nineteen years to revalidate the constitution along with all public debts is often viewed by scholars in a superficial manner, as, at best, a very weak check against tyranny. Yet, it is a "fundamental principle" of Jefferson's theory and what makes his theory unique. When this principle is placed inside a scheme where men are daily occupied in their public capacities and where they are in charge of their public and private lives, would a tyrannical situation develop to such an extent that a national convention would be the only solution? The permanent, periodic constitutional convention, rather than merely acting as a check against tyranny, is also a symbolic national recommitment of each citizen to every other citizen, as well as to the citizenry as a whole. Through daily action in the ward-republics, then, Jefferson thinks he has found a permanent check to tyranny, a way to keep alive the revolutionary ardor of the founding era, and a mechanism to allow the citizens truly to govern themselves. Given the centrality of the ward-republics to Jefferson's political philosophy, it is not hyperbole when he writes: "As Cato concluded every speech with the words, *Carthago delenda est*, so do I every opinion, with the injunction, 'divide the counties into wards.'"[28]

The ward-republic is the logical outgrowth of Jefferson's concept of man. His distrust of European canaille has already been noted; his faith in "the people" is manifest throughout his letters. In 1819 he writes to Spencer Roane: "Independence can be trusted nowhere but with the people in mass. They are inherently independent of all but moral law."[29] To John Adams he states that in "the multitude . . . vital elements of free government, of trial by jury, habeas corpus, freedom of the press, freedom of opinion, and representative government" are almost "innate."[30] And to William Findley he comments: "It is rare that the public sentiment decides immorally or unwisely, and the individual who differs from it ought to distrust and examine well his own opinion."[31] Self-governance is essential, vital, natural. "Every man, and every body of men on earth, possesses the right of self-government: they receive it with their being from the hand of nature."[32]

Of course, Jefferson's faith in the people to govern themselves is contingent upon their having both the information necessary for making intelligent decisions and the requisite education to employ the information usefully. From Paris in 1789 he claims that "wherever the people are well informed they can be trusted with their own government; that whenever things get so far wrong as to attract their notice, they may be relied on to set them to rights."[33] Concerning the second factor, he writes: "If we think them [i.e., the people] not enlightened enough to exercise their control with a wholesome discretion, the remedy is not to take it from them, but to inform their discretion by education."[34] General, state-funded education is also part of Jefferson's plan.

In a 1786 letter, Jefferson singles out education in his comments on the legal reforms that he helped to initiate in Virginia: "I think by far the most important bill in our whole code is that for the diffusion of knowledge among the people. No other sure foundation can be devised for the preservation of freedom, and happiness."[35] Much of Jefferson's lifework was expended in establishing a public school system for Virginia, the capstone of which was the creation of the University of Virginia.[36] Once more, the ward-republic is directly tied to his educational plans: that is, each ward-republic would also provide, at public expense, for the education of all inhabitants.

Before concluding our discussion of the role of politics in the political philosophy of Thomas Jefferson, it is necessary to return once more to Jefferson's concept of happiness. As has been explained, Jefferson rejects Locke's natural-rights claim to "life, liberty, and estate" in favor of "life, liberty, and the pursuit of happiness." And yet, to understand fully Jefferson's thoughts on this alteration, it is essential to make further distinctions between public and private happiness. It is important that in the opening passage of the Declaration of Independence, Jefferson prefers the more universal term *happiness* to the narrower and more popular *public happiness*—a phrase he has found felicitous two years earlier in a paper prepared for the Virginia Convention. *Public happiness* specifically refers to the citizen's right of access to the public realm where he can be free, can be seen, and can be, as Jefferson puts it, "a participator in public affairs."[37] That this public aspect of happiness is crucial to Jefferson can readily be seen in his writings on ward-republics, discussed above. However, Jefferson also believes in the pursuit of happiness in the private realm, outside the public gaze, "in the lap and love of my family, in the society of my neighbors and my books, in the wholesome occupations of my farm and my affairs."[38] The pursuit of happiness, in its dual interdependent facets, can provide a fully human life; but the pursuit of either at the neglect or expense of the other will lead to personal perversion in the individual and to social decay in the corporate body. Because his grand vision of a society of ward-republics has yet to be implemented, the sole avenue for Americans to pursue happiness has been restricted to the private realm, which, even in Jefferson's day, was increasingly becoming synonymous with the market. Because the public arena was reserved exclusively for the few, most men could find only a limited, partial happiness in the private realm and, because of this, would live less than fully human lives.

To understand further Jefferson's atavistic views of the political, it is helpful for us to look at the civic-humanist tradition. As Pocock explains it: "Civic humanism denotes a style of thought . . . in which it is contended that the development of the individual towards self-fulfillment is possible only when the individual acts as a citizen, that is as a conscious and autonomous participant in an autonomous decision-taking political community, the polis or republic."[39] The roots of civic humanism are as old as Western political philosophy itself. "Part Aristotle, part Cicero, part Machiavelli," writes Isaac Kramnick, "civic humanism conceives of man as a political being whose realization of self occurs only through participation in public life, through active citizenship in a republic."[40] While Jefferson argues for the necessity of creating a public space in which all men will be able to participate in politics, will rule and be ruled, he is also aware of the tension between the *vita activa* and the *vita contemplativa*.

> Since the time of Plato and Aristotle, the question had been intermittently discussed of the relative merits of a life spent in social activity—the *vita activa*—and a life spent in philosophical pursuit of pure knowledge—the *vita contemplativa*. To Athenians . . . the problem of whether politics and philosophy were not antithetical had been a painful one. The medieval mind had, of course, loaded the debate in favor of contemplation; . . . But in later Florentine thinking there is a great deal said in favor of a *vita activa* which is specifically a *vivere civile*—a way of life given over to civic concerns and the (ultimately political) activity of citizenship.[41]

Two important points should not be overlooked in Jefferson's theory of politics. First, although man is a political creature and the *vita activa* is part of a human life, Jefferson, like Aristotle in his *Nicomachean Ethics*, considers the *vita contemplativa* to be the highest human activity. He urges scientist and philosopher David Rittenhouse to eschew politics for work in the laboratory. After Jefferson notes that he is aware of "the obligation" that an individual has toward government, he writes that he is "also satisfied there is an order of geniusses above that obligation, & therefore exempted from it, no body can conceive that nature ever intended to throw away a Newton upon occupations of a crown."[42] Rittenhouse and Franklin would be able to serve humanity better by pursuing philosophy. This notion that there are a few rare individuals who, by virtue of their genius, are exempt from government service is tied to Jefferson's belief that society cannot require any individual to serve it perpetually. Declining an invitation to return to the political life of Richmond, Jefferson tells James Monroe that thirteen years of public service have given him a "right to withdraw" from politics. Service to the state has to have limits, otherwise "nothing could so completely divest us of that liberty as the establishment of the opinion that the state has a *perpetual* right to the services of all it's members." A balance, therefore, has to be reached between the public and the private: "If we are made in some degree for others, yet in a greater degree are we made for ourselves."[43] It is not a matter of finding fulfillment in one arena or the other, for both are crucial to the pursuit of happiness; and even a genius like Rittenhouse would still participate in the community through the ward-republics.

This dichotomy of happiness in public and in private spheres can be seen in Jefferson's writings on Epictetus, Epicurus, and Jesus Christ.[44] Although Jefferson's knowledge of ancient philosophy was broad, if not always accurate, it is the doctrines of Epictetus, Epicurus, and Christ that Jefferson believes come closest to expressing his own moral beliefs. In each case, Jefferson is adamant that it is the original unadulterated teachings of the masters that are worthy of emulation, not the bastardizations that have been handed down by their disciples and followers.[45] Epicurus provides key precepts for the attainment of happiness by the individual who has been removed from the public realm; Christ supplies the necessary complement, those moral laws that are to guide a man's actions as a social being; and Epictetus is, more or less, a synthesis of the two.

Throughout his life, Jefferson took careful notes concerning those things which he found of particular interest. These notes range from colorful and vivid accounts of his wanderings throughout Europe to brief summaries of the philosophies of men whose works he has read. In a letter to William Short in 1819, Jefferson offers his "Syllabus of the Doctrines of Epicurus." This short list echoes much of Jefferson's own philosophy: "Happiness the aim of life. Virtue the foundation of happiness. Utility the test of virtue." The *telos* of human life is happiness founded on virtue, which consists of "1. Prudence. 2. Temperance. 3. Fortitude. 4. Justice. To which are opposed, 1. Folly. 2. Desire. 3. Fear. 4. Deceit."[46] The reward of a life lived in accordance with virtue is pleasure, which to Epicurus is twofold: kinetic and katastematic.[47] Jefferson labels these "active and in-do-lent": the latter is the absence of pain; the former is agreeable, harmonious motion.[48] This striving for pleasure is innate, natural. Tranquility, moreover, is the *"summum bonum."* Since the avoidance of pain is a prerequisite to tranquility, Epicurus advocates a total avoidance of politics, because the costs of a public existence are too great, the risks too high. But the apolitical base of Epicurus's thought does not preclude one from the close social relationship of friendship. Indeed, friendship is an important component to happiness in that it provides a stabilizing hedge against an uncertain, often cruel world; it also allows man the opportunity of showing benevolence toward others, which for Epicurus is more pleasurable than receiving it. To obtain genuine, lasting pleasure, friendship must be a complete commitment to others, which requires man to love his friends to the same degree as he loves himself.[49] Throughout Jefferson's years of public service as governor of Virginia, minister to France, and president of the United States, he longed for the tranquility of life at Monticello: a style of life that he envisioned as being filled with warmth, love, and friendship, where simple ideas, pleasures, and concerns could be freely exchanged without fear of the uncertainties of the larger world.

The radically apolitical individualism of Epicurus is evident, and for this reason Jefferson cannot be considered a strict Epicurean. Along with Epicurus, Jefferson believes that man is a free agent; but unlike his teacher, he views man also as a social being who has a moral duty to engage in politics.[50] Although this tour of service to the community has time limits which no society has a right to invade, every man has to meet his public responsibilities before he can withdraw to the domestic tranquility of his primary social group. In the teachings of Jesus, Jefferson locates the necessary social complement to Epicurus.

On more than one occasion Jefferson proclaims himself to be "a *real Christian*, that is to say, a disciple of the doctrines of Jesus, very different from the Platonists, who call *me* infidel and *themselves* Christians and preachers of the gospel, while they draw all their characteristic dogmas from what its author never said nor saw."[51] Being careful to distinguish what are authentically the teachings of Jesus from "the rubbish in which it is buried," Jefferson believes that the doctrines of Jesus provide "a system of the most sublime morality which has ever fallen from the lips of man."[52] Jefferson's choice of words in the last sentence accurately reflects his Christianity. Scientist, philosopher, and child of the Enlightenment, Jefferson has little respect for the theological debates of his day: questions concerning the trinity, transubstantiation, and the immaculate conception are too metaphysical for his tastes. His own unshakeable faith in scientific progress and the gradual enlightenment of man leads him to predict that "the day will come when the mystical generation of Jesus, by the supreme being as his father in the womb of a virgin will be classed with the fable of the generation of Minerva in the brain of Jupiter."[53]

While enjoying the peace of Monticello during his twilight years, Jefferson writes a synopsis of the doctrines of Jesus, each of which, he maintains, tends to the happiness of man. In three short sentences, Jefferson believes he has encapsulated the essence of true Christianity:

1. That there is one only God, and he all perfect.
2. That there is a future state of rewards and punishments.
3. That to love God with all thy heart and thy neighbor as thyself, is the sum of religion.[54]

The last point, taken from the Sermon on the Mount, is of utmost importance in Jefferson's writings.[55] He believes that these simple precepts establish a "universal philanthropy, not only to kindred and friends, to neighbors and countrymen, but to all mankind, gathering all into one family, under the bonds of love, charity, peace, common wants and common aids."[56] Mankind is one family, held together, not out of a sense of fear or egotistical self-interest, but by "bonds of love, charity, peace, common wants and common aids." Unlike most of his contemporaries, Jefferson views the gathering of men into communities to be natural, to be in accordance with the laws of heaven, and to be good in and of itself. Indeed, Jefferson perceives order, harmony, and purpose in the very nature of the universe. Beyond the teachings of an extraordinary man called Christ, Jefferson has no doubts concerning either the existence or the rational planning of a supreme creator. Again, an empirical scientist whose own personal trinity was composed of Newton, Bacon, and Locke, Jefferson writes:

> On the contrary I hold (without appeal to revelation) that when we take a view of the Universe, in it's parts general or particular, it is impossible for the human mind not to percieve and feel a conviction of design, consummate skill, and indefinite power in every atom of its composition. The movements of the heavenly bodies, so exactly held in their course by the balance of centrifugal and centripetal forces, the structure of our earth itself, with it's distribution of lands, waters and atmosphere, animal and vegetable bodies, examined in all their minutest particles, insects mere atoms of life, yet as perfectly organised as man or mammoth, the mineral substances, their generation and uses, it is impossible, I say, for the human mind not to believe that there is, in all this, design, cause and effect, up to an ultimate cause, a fabricator of all things from matter and motion, their preserver and regulator while permitted to exist in their present forms, and their regenerator into new and other forms.[57]

Given this blending of the social and the individual, of Christ and Epicurus, it is understandable that at least one scholar has claimed, albeit mistakenly, that Aristotle's concept of eudemonism is closer to symbolizing Jefferson than is the hedonism of Epicurus.[58] Here is where the Stoic Epictetus enters Jefferson's system by attempting to bring order and harmony to both the personal and the political, with eudemonia as the result. In contrast to Epicurus, the Stoic considers that it is an aspect of his duty to be part of the public realm, because it, too, is an integral part of life. Epictetus, like Jefferson, also believes in an innate moral predisposition that allows men to live in community; unlike Christ, Epictetus's teachings do not have an otherworldly tone about them. Epictetus, then, presents a middle ground between Epicurus and Christ, once again emphasizing the necessity of both the public and the private realms.

Jefferson's views on politics, then, were also out of step with those of most of his contemporaries. While many theorists and politicians wanted to keep "the people" out of the political process, Jefferson felt it to be crucial—for both the individual and the community—that all citizens become intimately involved in public life. Still, a life that is totally devoted to others will be as impoverished as a life that is devoted entirely to self. It is through activity in both the public and the private arenas that man can pursue genuine happiness and live the Jeffersonian good life. Men, therefore, have a right not to be excluded from pursuing happiness in either realm; indeed, they must be encouraged to pursue happiness in both.

6

Jefferson in the American Context: The Liberalism of Madison and Hamilton

If the morality of one man produces a just line of conduct in him, acting individually, why should not the morality of one hundred men produce a just line of conduct in them, acting together?

—Jefferson

Had every Athenian citizen been a Socrates, every Athenian assembly would still have been a mob.

—Madison

Why has government been instituted at all? Because the passions of men will not conform to the dictates of reason and justice, without constraint. Has it been found that bodies of men act with more rectitude or greater disinterestedness than individuals? The contrary of this has been inferred by all accurate observers of the conduct of mankind.[1]

—Hamilton

To define the political philosophy of Thomas Jefferson aright, it is necessary to place him back within the overall context of American political thought during the founding era. When placed against the bland and colorless backdrop portrayed by the consensus historians, it becomes possible to appreciate fully not only the uniqueness of Jefferson's political philosophy but also its presence as a legitimate alternative to American liberalism. This objective can be successfully accomplished by comparing Jefferson's political theory primarily to that of James Madison, principal architect of the Constitution, and tangentially to Alexander Hamilton, Madison's coauthor of *The Federalist* and chief articulator of the dream of American capitalism.[2]

The relationship between Jefferson and Madison has been the subject of many historical studies. The two Virginians are often presented as close personal friends and political allies, engaged in what Adrienne Koch has called "the great collaboration" of nation building, as well as in the battle against Alexander Hamilton's centralized government. Such a perspective, however, is mistaken. Although Jefferson and Madison were indeed friends and allies, it was Hamilton and Madison who "collaborated" on the founding of the American state. From the Annapolis and Philadelphia conventions through the ratification debates and *The Federalist*, it was Madison and Hamilton who forged "the great collaboration," while Jefferson's energies were being diverted in Paris. Even though a brief perusal of Madison's works will indicate their similarity to those of Hamilton, this is not to say that their theories are one and the same. After Jefferson's return to America, a democratic-pastoral touch occasionally surfaces in Madison. Still, in his concept of property, man, government, and society, Madison is closer to Hamilton than to Jefferson.[3] It is the first of these concepts, property, to which my analysis first turns.

It is relatively well known that Madison believed that "Government is instituted and ought to be exercised for the benefit of the people; which consists in the enjoyment of life and liberty, with the right of acquiring and using property, and generally of pursuing and obtaining happiness and safety."[4] The protection of property and rights Madison mentions on countless occasions as the end of government; it is one of the few subjects to which Madison offers anything even remotely resembling a systematic treatment.[5]

In 1792, in a Philadelphia-based publication called the *National Gazette*, Madison wrote an article entitled "Property." In this essay, Madison employs Blackstone and explains that the term *property*, in its "particular application," means "that dominion which one man claims and exercises over the external things of the world, in exclusion of every other individual." This is, obviously, a conventional definition of property. But Madison continues his essay: "In its larger and juster meaning, it [property] embraces everything to which a man may attach a value and have a right, and *which leaves to every one else the like advantage."* Hence, a man's "land, or merchandise, or money," as well as his "opinions," may be considered to be a part of his property. Furthermore, a man also has "property in the free use of his faculties, and free choice of the objects on which to employ them."[6] Madison plainly gives the term *property* considerable breadth; and government, it must be remembered, "is instituted to protect property of every sort." It is interesting that Madison, within this ample definition of property, maintains, as did Locke and Hobbes, that there is an explicit property hierarchy wherein "conscience" and "free use of faculties" rank higher than property in the "particular" (i.e., "external things of the world") sense of the term. Madison writes: "Conscience is the most sacred of all property. . . . To guard a man's house as his castle, to pay public and enforce private debts with the most exact faith, can give no title to invade a man's conscience, which is more sacred than his castle."[7] Madison continues:

> That is not a just government, nor is property secure under it, where arbitrary restrictions, exemptions, and monopolies deny to part of its citizens that free use of their faculties and free choice of their occupations which not only constitute their property in the general sense of the word, but are the means of acquiring property strictly so called.[8]

Madison notes that the general right of property is a necessary prerequisite to the "particular right"; however, he fails to demonstrate, at least explicitly in this essay, any awareness that the very establishment of the particular property rights may, after a certain point in a society's economic development, forever preclude the right of property in the "general" and "juster" sense for a certain class of citizens. Momentarily, in another of Madison's writings, it will become clear that he does see the inevitable tension created out of this apparent dilemma; but he believes that it is a "fact of life" and therefore cannot be remedied.[9] Before pursuing this topic into a fuller analysis of its political implications, a discussion of Madison's concept of man is needed.

Madison's concept of man can readily be located in *The Federalist*. It is both important and interesting to note that the entire body of papers, though primarily coauthored with Hamilton, is signed by one person, Publius. As Martin Diamond has persuasively argued, the collection can be read, then, as the work of one theorist—rather than two.[10] And at the time of publication, the two were, indeed, as one.

Recently the authorship of each paper has been determined, so that particular insights may be drawn. With the exception of "Federalist 6," Madison writes most of the papers dealing with the nature of man; making Hamilton's concept of man at times look almost angelic. Not surprisingly, Hamilton is most comfortable writing those papers, erected upon Madison's concept of man, that concern commerce, industry, and government.

James Madison, as author of the famous "Tenth Federalist," was concerned with the disruptive tendencies of factions. Indeed, it was the ability to control factions that Madison felt was the real genius in the American scheme of government. Madison understands a faction to be "a number of citizens, whether amounting to a majority or minority of the whole, who are united and actuated by some common impulse of passion, or of interest, adverse to the rights of other citizens, or to the permanent and aggregate interests of the community."[11] By making a careful analysis of the roots of faction, an initial glimpse into Madison's concept of man can be obtained.

A comparative-historic study of the past has made it poignantly evident to Madison, as it has to Hamilton, that "the diseases of factions" have proved "fatal to other popular governments." Moreover, the recent revolts in North Carolina and Pennsylvania, and Shays' Rebellion, which Madison characterizes as an "alarming sympton," have served only to buttress his fears over the probable spread of the disease in the United States.[12] Madison believes that "the latent causes of faction are thus sown in the nature of man." More specifically he believes that factions result from the "diversity in the faculties of men, from which the rights of property originate."[13] Although the different faculties of men are the causes of these dangerous factions, "the protection of these faculties is the first object of government."[14] Hence, they are beyond the scope of government intervention.

Indeed, Madison first notes two theoretical ways of removing the causes of factions—namely, (1) "destroying the liberty which is essential to its existence," and (2) "giving to every citizen the same opinions, the same passions, and the same interests"; then he specifically rejects either mode, believing the former cure to the violent factions to have been "worse than the disease" itself, whereas the latter is "impracticable."[15] Madison sees the obvious result of this protection of man's faculties: "From the protection of different and unequal faculties of acquiring property, the possession of different degrees and kinds of property immediately results: and from the influence of these on the sentiments and views of the respective proprietors ensues a division of society into different interests and parties."[16] To Madison, then, the "most common and durable source of factions has been the various and unequal distribution of property," which is the result of the "diversity in the faculties of men."[17] Through Jefferson's proposal of giving every male fifty acres of land and through his legislation against entail and primogeniture, along with his principle that the earth belongs to the living, he believes that he can combat the serious antisocial consequences resulting from inequality of property. This Madison is unwilling to do. Consequently, Madison views the politicosocial landscape as an inevitable panorama of separate, antagonistic interests.

> Those who hold, and those who are without property, have ever formed distinct interests in society. Those who are creditors, and those who are debtors, fall under a like discrimination. A landed interest, a manufacturing interest, a mercantile interest, a monied interest, with many lesser interests, grow up of necessity in civilized nations, and divide them into different classes, actuated by different sentiments and views. The regulation of these various and interfering interests forms the principal task of modern Legislation.[18]

101

At first glance, the antagonisms resulting from property differences seem to be the sole cause of domestic unrest. But on closer examination, it can be seen that to Madison the root of man's antisocial condition runs far deeper. Beyond property divisions run other causes of animosity. In his boldest statement on this point, Madison writes:

> A zeal for different opinions concerning religion, concerning Government . . . have in turn divided mankind into parties, inflamed them with mutual animosity, and rendered them much more disposed to vex and oppress each other, than to co-operate for their common good. So strong is this propensity of mankind to fall into mutual animosities, that where no substantial occasion presents itself, the most frivolous and fanciful distinctions have been sufficient to kindle their unfriendly passions, and excite their most violent conflicts.[19]

In view of this quotation it is small wonder, then, in "Federalist 51," in tones that would have been harmonious sounding to Hobbes, Madison reiterates what Arthur O. Lovejoy aptly refers to as "the method of counterpoise": "Ambition must be made to counteract ambition. . . . It may be a reflection on human nature that such devices should be necessary. . . . But what is government itself but the greatest of all reflections on human nature? If men were angels, no government would be necessary."[20] As I have previously demonstrated, Jefferson clearly believes that in some types of societies, "no government would be necessary." Obviously, the sober Madison feels much more secure with Hamilton's well-known position on man—that is, he holds mankind in pragmatic distrust. Because of ignorance, selfishness, and an absence of self-control, men are incapable of self-government. "A vast majority of mankind," Hamilton writes, "is entirely biased by motives of self-interest."[21] "A fondness for power is implanted in most men, and it is natural to abuse it when acquired."[22] Hamilton observes other antisocial passions: ambition, rapacity, avarice, and vindictiveness, to name but a few.[23]

To summarize, these quotations from "Federalist 10" and "Federalist 51" are among Madison's more pessimistic statements on the nature of man. Even if property could be evenly distributed, which Madison would never concede, men would still be at each other's throats over "the most frivolous and fanciful distinctions." Given this "realist" perspective, some form of government—a leviathan, a monster—becomes necessary to maintain order and to control the antisocial characteristics of man.

If the Madisonian concept of man seems close to that of David Hume, do not be surprised: as the noted historian Douglass Adair has shown, Madison, like Hamilton, was a student of Hume's works. While at Princeton, Madison studied under Dr. John W. Witherspoon, who had studied both David Hume and Adam Smith. In Hume's writings, Madison (and Hamilton) find a rich source of practical, "common-sense" solutions to the problems of factions. The similarity of their views can readily be seen in several of Hume's works: especially in his "Parties" and "Idea of a Perfect Commonwealth." In the former, like Madison of "Federalist 10," and Hamilton of "Federalist 9," Hume finds a natural tendency of men to separate into factions. "Men have such a propensity to divide into personal factions," he writes, "that the smallest appearance of real difference will produce them."[24] In the latter Humean exposition, Madison finds his "republican remedy for the diseases most incident to republican government."[25] At the end of "Idea of a Perfect Commonwealth," Hume casually but thoroughly demolishes the small-republic theory of Montesquieu. Hume classifies it as a "falsehood of the common opinion, that no large state, such as France or Great Britain, could ever be modelled into a commonwealth, but that such a form of government can only take place in a small city or territory." To Hume the very opposite seems to be true. "Though it is more difficult to form a republican government in an extensive country than in a city; there is more facility, when once it is formed, of preserving it steady and uniform, without tumult and faction."[26] Hume then presents both Madison and Hamilton with the cure for the diseases of factions:

> In a large government, which is modelled with masterly skill, there is compass and room enough to refine the democracy, from the lower people, who may be admitted into the first elections or first concoction of the commonwealth, to the higher magistrates, who direct all the movements. At the same time, the parts are so distant and remote, that it is very difficult, either by intrigue, prejudice, or passion, to hurry them into any measures against the public interest.[27]

Obviously, this is quite close to Madison's "Federalist 10," in which he remarks:

> Extend the sphere, and you take in a greater variety of parties and interests; you make it less probable that a majority of the whole will have a common motive to invade the rights of other citizens; or if such a common motive exists, it will be more difficult for all who feel it to discover their own strength, and to act in unison with each other.[28]

And in "Federalist 51" he states:

> Whilst all authority in it [the United States government] will be derived from and dependent on the society, the society itself will be broken into so many parts, interests and classes of citizens, that the rights of individuals or of the minority, will be in little danger from interested combinations of the majority.[29]

It can be concluded that Madison found in Hume the germ of his own scheme of extended government.

Up to this point, Madison appears to be almost a pure Hamiltonian. There appears in Madison's writings, nevertheless, a touch of Jeffersonian humanism, as reflected in his views on suffrage and the ideal citizen.

Madison's views on suffrage changed several times during his lengthy career. From the start, Madison is fully aware that the right of suffrage is a question of "great delicacy" and of "critical importance." In a letter on the Kentucky Constitution, dated 23 August 1785, Madison outlines the options available to the legislators. "To restrain [suffrage] to the land holders will in time exclude too great a proportion of citizens." And yet, Madison warns that "to extend it to all citizens without regard to property, or even to all who possess a pittance may throw too much power into hands which will either abuse it themselves or sell it to the rich who will abuse it." On this occasion of Kentucky's Constitutional Convention, he offers a typical Madisonian compromise: "I have thought it might be a good middle course to narrow this right in the choice of the least popular, & to enlarge it in that of the more popular branch of the Legislature."[30]

Two years later, in Philadelphia, Madison presents a different view on the suffrage issue. In a convention speech on 7 August 1787, he rose to make a tentative recommendation that there be a property qualification for electors to the House of Representatives. In the language of a practical politician, Madison cautions the convention that "whether the Constitutional qualification ought to be a freehold" will certainly depend "on the probable reception such a change would meet in States where the right was now exercised by every description of people." With the appropriate words of warning being given, Madison then confesses that "viewing the subject in its merits alone, the freeholders of the Country would be the safest depositories of Republican liberty."[31] And in an earlier convention speech on suffrage qualifications in the Senate, Madison advocates that the "land-holders ought to have a share in the government, to support" their "invaluable interests." The voting pattern must be drawn up, he states, "to protect the minority of the opulent against the majority.[32] While no property qualification for voters or officeholders appears in the body of the Constitution, a motion was carried at the convention, instructing a committee to fix property qualifications for voting. The committee failed to agree upon the nature of the qualifications to be imposed, and the issue was dropped.[33]

Unable to reach an agreement on voting qualifications, the convention set some guidelines and then returned the question to the individual states. But it must be remembered that voting was an issue only with regard to the House of Representatives: the other three controlling bodies—namely, the Senate, the executive, and the Supreme Court—were removed from direct popular control. With regard to the House, voting qualifications were fixed by the convention at the standards of the individual states: "The House of Representatives shall be composed of members chosen every second year by the people of the several states, and the electors in each state shall have the qualifications requisite for electors of the most numerous branch of the state legislature."[34]

In light of this sentence, Madison writes in "Federalist 57":

> Who are to be the electors of the federal representatives? Not the rich, more than the poor; not the learned, more than the ignorant; not the haughty heirs of distinguished names, more than the humble sons of obscurity and unpropitious fortune. The electors are to be the great body of the people of the United States. They are to be the same who exercise the right in every State of electing the corresponding branch of the legislature of the State.[35]

And with regard to the qualifications necessary for running for office in the House of Representatives, Madison, in "Federalist 52," writes:

> A representative of the United States must be of the age of twenty-five years; must have been seven years a citizen of the United States; must . . . be an inhabitant of the State he is to represent; and, during the time of his service, must be in no office under the United States. Under these reasonable limitations, the door of this part of the federal government is open to merit of every description, whether native or adoptive, whether young or old, and without regard to poverty or wealth, or to any particular profession of religious faith.[36]

What, from these quotations, appears to be a set of relatively egalitarian voting measures, devoid of property qualifications, is anything but that. Madison, furthermore, is not ignorant of this fact. In "Federalist 54" he states: " 'The qualifications on which the right of suffrage depend are not, perhaps, the same in any two States. In some of the States the difference is very material. In every State, a certain proportion of inhabitants are deprived of this right by the constitution of the State.'"[37] Exactly what this means in actual figures of disenfranchisement is difficult to tell. Historians, though they disagree on numbers, agree that all states had property-owning or tax-paying qualifications. For example, in Massachusetts, suffrage was granted to all white males who owned an estate with an annual income of three pounds or a total value of sixty pounds; Massachusetts had an even higher qualification with regard to its senate.[38]

Later on in his life, after Jefferson's return from France, it appears that Madison had second thoughts on his position during the convention era. Sometime during the year 1821, while correcting and expanding his own convention notes from other recently printed accounts of the Constitutional Convention, Madison records a modest—but highly significant—change in his views on voting. Commenting on his convention speech of August 7, he notes: "These observations (in the speech of J.M. See debates in the Convention of 1787 on the [7] day of [August]) do not convey the speaker's more full & matured view of the subject, which is subjoined. He felt too much at the time the example of Virginia."[39] While he was content with his freeholder's position in 1787, now, more than three decades later, Madison explicitly rejects any voting conditions that would, either now or in the future, exclude the mass of society from political representation. It should be briefly mentioned before turning to his exact proposal on voting, that this changing by Madison of his convention notes is one of only a handful of corrections he made; that suffrage is a question on which he feels compelled to alter his views shows the degree of concern that Madison felt over this issue.

In the 1821 revision of his position at the convention, Madison warns: "Allow the right [of suffrage] exclusively to property, and the rights of persons may be oppressed. . . . Extend it equally to all, and the rights of property or the claims of justice may be overruled by a majority without property, or interested in measures of injustice."[40] Madison then reviews several hypothetical schemes on which qualification for suffrage could be based. He rejects a property qualification for voting on the grounds that "it violates the vital principle of free Government that those who are to be bound by laws, ought to have a voice in making them. And the violation would be more strikingly unjust as the lawmakers become the minority."[41] Madison then reviews several voting schemes.

After rejecting two limited-franchise options, Madison endorses a third: in tones similar to his original suffrage speeches at the Constitutional Convention of 1787, Madison's third option of "Confining the right of electing one Branch of the Legislature to freeholders, and admitting all others to a common right with holders of property, in electing the other Branch" receives a most favorable review. Indeed, Madison believes this option can be implemented until "the non freeholders should be the majority."[42]

However, in the final analysis, faced with the unrelenting rise of a propertyless class, Madison is forced to accept the only alternative left. He writes:

> Under every view of the subject, it seems indispensable that the Mass of Citizens should not be without a voice, in making the laws which they are to obey, & in chusing the Magistrates, who are to administer them, and if the only alternative be between an equal & universal right of suffrage for each branch of the Government and a confinement of the *entire* right to a part of the Citizens, it is better that those having the greater interest at stake namely that of property & persons both, should be deprived of half their share in the Government; than, that those having the lesser interest, that of personal rights only, should be deprived of the whole.[43]

Hardly a ringing exultation in support of universal suffrage as proposed by Jefferson, it does, nevertheless, show that Madison clearly sees that any attempt to restrict suffrage in any manner whatever will ultimately fail to meet the "revolutions" he foresees in "Federalist 41."

A Jeffersonian flavor also surfaces whenever Madison discusses the individual removed from the influences of the group. As an isolated individual, Madison sees man as "timid and cautious," a "reasonable" creature.[44] It is as a member of a group, a class, or a faction that the individual, surrounded by like-minded individuals, "acquires firmness and confidence in proportion to the number with which [he] is associated."[45] As an isolated individual, man is timid; as a member of a group, he becomes unreasonable, and passion rules the day. Government, hence, cannot rely solely on reason to rule, because passion will usually, if not always, hold sway. Madison dramatically illustrates this point in "Federalist 55," where he claims: "Had every Athenian citizen been a Socrates, every Athenian assembly would still have been a mob."[46] His views on the farmer are also illustrative.

It is important to notice that Madison, like Jefferson before him, believes that the "husbandman" is the firmest base for republican government. Indeed, the "husbandman" is also Madison's archetypal ideal citizen. After Jefferson's return to the United States, Madison states in a 1792 newspaper article on the question of the best distribution for a republican government:

> The life of the husbandman is pre-eminently suited to the comfort and happiness of the individual. *Health,* the first of blessings, is an appertenance of his property and his employment. *Virtue,* the health of the soul, is another part of his patrimony, and no less favored by his situation. *Intelligence* may be cultivated in this as well as in any other walk of life. If the mind be less susceptible of polish in retirement than in a crowd, it is more capable of profound and comprehensive efforts. . . . *Competency* is more universally the lot of those who dwell in the country where liberty is at the same time their lot. The extremes, both of want and of waste, have other abodes. 'Tis not the country that peoples either the Bridewells or the Bedlams. These mansions of wretchedness are tenanted from the distresses and vices of overgrown cities.[47]

The mark of Jefferson is manifest. Cities are breeding grounds for decay, while farms cultivate virtue. Echoing James Harrington, Adam Smith, and Jefferson, Madison writes:

> The class of citizens who provide at once their own food and their own raiment, may be viewed as the most truly inde-

pendent and happy. They are more; they are the best basis of public liberty and the strongest bulwark of public safety. It follows, that the greater the proportion of this class to the whole society, the more free, the more independent, and the more happy must be the society itself.[48]

It follows that Madison does not always view labor as a necessary evil which all men had to suffer in order to sustain themselves. Rather, it appears that to Madison, labor—in the above form—has intrinsic values—for example, health, virtue, intelligence, and competency. This position is understandable, for it is the coming of industrialization, with its side effects of "Bridewells" and "Bedlams," that is a cause of tremendous apprehension to Madison, as it is to Jefferson.

Seeing the almost inevitable rise of manufacturing and of class antagonisms, Madison ends his article on a rather somber note:

> In appreciating the regular branches of manufacturing and mechanical industry, their tendency must be compared with the principles laid down, and their merit graduated accordingly. Whatever is least favorable to vigor of body, to the faculties of the mind, or to the virtues or to the utilities of life, instead of being forced or fostered by public authority, ought to be seen with regret, as long as occupations more friendly to human happiness lie vacant.[49]

Prior to the termination of Jefferson's ministry in France, such "optimistic" perspectives are absent in Madison. Even so, it would be misleading to claim that these passages are representative of Madison, for they are not. Instead, Madison is always cautious, prudential, and "fearful." It is his constant concern over the twin evils of the inevitable decline of the republic and the advance of corruption produced by commercial modernity itself that gives Madisonian rhetoric the style and tone of the country half of the court-country paradigm of the republican tradition. Drew McCoy carefully summarizes Madison's realism: "If the republican revolution had initially been defined as an escape from time, Madison had always acknowledged that, in the long run, such a revolution was doomed. Eventually the New World would come to resemble the Old."[50]

110

Even before the 1792 article, Madison is concerned with the emerging problems of overpopulation and unemployment. He warns Jefferson that "a certain degree of misery seems inseparable from a high degree of populousness." In 1821 the elder Madison comments that he is relieved that the United States has what he calls a "precious advantage" in the "actual distribution of property particularly the landed property; and in the universal hope of acquiring property."[51] As late as the end of the first quarter of the nineteenth century, thanks primarily to the Louisiana Purchase, American men had the hope and opportunity to own land. In this fact, Madison, like Jefferson, finds the "happiest contrasts" of the position of the United States to "that of the old world."[52] And yet, Madison is aware that time is running out on this "precious advantage," because of the pressures of a rising population and a decreasing quantity of unowned land. As early as The Federalist, Madison shows that he believes that there will eventually be an exodus from farming to manufacturing:

> As long as agriculture continues the sole field of labour, the importation of manufactures must increase as the consumers multiply. As soon as domestic manufactures are begun by the hands not called for by agriculture, the imported manufactures will decrease as the numbers of people increase. In a more remote stage, the imports may consist in considerable part of raw materials, which will be wrought into articles for exportation, and will, therefore, require rather the encouragement of bounties than to be loaded with discouraging duties. A system of Government meant for duration ought to contemplate these revolutions and be able to accommodate itself to them.[53]

By 1827 Madison has sharpened his perspective on the problem, and in a letter to a friend he plainly declares himself to be a Malthusian. Madison realizes that "the sudden introduction of labour-saving machinery, taking employment from those who labour," is another cause of serious concern. Where Hamilton happily envisions a boon to manufacturing as a result of the decrease in the cost of production, Madison sees a vicious circle. He sees a "constant tendency of an increase" in the laboring population after "the increase of food has reached its term." This, he believes, will aggravate "the competition for employment" and thereby will reduce "wages to their minimum, and privation to its maximum."[54] With an increasing number of men being reduced to "the bare necessaries of life,"[55] it is all too clear to Madison that the "evil proceeding from this tendency" has to be checked by "either physical or moral causes." However, to a man who believes that government was instituted to protect men's "diverse faculties," to protect their "free use of faculties," and to "protect property," such "checks are themselves but so many evils." Confronted with this Gordian knot, Madison resignedly laments: "With this knowledge of the impossibility of banishing evil altogether from human society, we must console ourselves with the belief that it is overbalanced by the good mixed with it."[56]

Given this concept of man, which views him as being ultimately contentious, it follows that Madison also should be an advocate of strong government. Yet, it must be remembered that Madison perceives every man to be quarrelsome: "Had *every* Athenian citizen been a Socrates, *every* Athenian assembly would still have been a mob." Government by men, consequently, must be built on the basis of ambition counteracting ambition. Hamilton's powerful, virtually unlimited government relies too heavily on humans; less subject to human frailty, Madison feels that a better solution can be found in a mechanical system of government, employing nonhuman factors wherever possible. Through an extended republic, itself divided into several states composed of numerous counties, with each component having a degree of power, Madison is sure that he can stall the movement of all but the most intense factions, and thereby provide for equilibrium. The division of the government into three branches, moreover, each of which is one step further removed from the people, provides an additional safeguard. Limited suffrage and Edmund Burke's model of representation provide additional checks. The point is that Madison is striving to build a machinelike system, a structure of government that will automatically divert and diffuse factions; furthermore, the system will check itself by not allowing its human operators to become too powerful. It will be a self-perpetuating government, with Madison as the immortal father, controlling society from beyond the grave. This is precisely the sort of government that Jefferson fears. In contrast, Hamilton believes that vigorous, strong government, though risky, is the only method for thwarting factions while actively pursuing empire. Still, both Madison and Hamilton are in accord with the idea that the need for an effective sovereign is built into the very nature of man.[57]

Although Hamilton's writings on government and man provide considerable insight into the similarities in his and Madison's political theories, it is from Hamilton's works on manufacturing, industry, and banking that the real Hamilton distinctively emerges. Had Max Weber never heard of Benjamin Franklin, Weber's essay *The Protestant Ethic and the Spirit of Capitalism* could just as profitably have used Hamilton as the herald for the new ethos of capitalism.[58] In almost all of Hamilton's political writings there is a sense of urgency to skim over what he assumes to be the obvious components of the nature of man and government, the lessons of history, et cetera, and to move to the crucial area of political economy.[59] Once there, Hamilton spares no ink in spelling out his unique dream of power, wealth, and empire.

Hamilton's economic plan has three parts: assumption of the debt, creation of a national bank, and active encouragement of manufacturing. To increase the "active capital" of the United States is his first concern.[60] By funding the debt from the Revolutionary War at par value, Hamilton hopes to assure foreign and domestic investors that their money is secure—and though reduced from 6 percent to 4 percent, is still providing a handsome return—in the new nation. Simultaneously, through the establishment of a national bank, he wants to create a large capital fund to aid industries. In his official report to the Congress on the national bank, he argues that the principal advantage that would accrue to the nation from the bank would be "the augmentation of the active or productive capital."[61] After all, Hamilton considers "money" to be "the vital principle of the body politic; as that which sustains its life and motion, and enables it to perform its most essential functions."[62] Hamilton explains that "the money, which a merchant keeps in his chest, waiting for a favorable opportunity to employ it, produces nothing"; and yet, when placed in a bank, "it acquires life, or, in other words, an active and productive quality."[63] With this pool of capital, claims Vernon Parrington, Hamilton wants to link "the interest of the State in an intimate connection with those of the rich individuals belonging to it."[64] In time, the bank will become part of the political machinery: "It is to be considered that such a bank is not a mere matter of private property, but a political machine of the greatest importance to the state."[65]

The third part of the Hamiltonian design is the active encouragement of manufacturing by the government. In the most brilliant of the famous *Reports*, he patiently and persuasively argues for capitalism. Shrewdly he begins with a veiled attack on the physiocratic view of farming: "It ought readily to be conceded that the cultivation of the earth . . . has intrinsically a strong claim to preeminence over every other kind of industry." Immediately, he takes the offensive: "But, that it has a title to anything like an exclusive predilection, in any country, ought to be admitted with great caution."[66] From here, he proceeds to attack laissez-faire economics and to offer his reasons for the need for government to stimulate industry.

Among the more idiosyncratic reasons is his claim that even a careless, lazy farmer can obtain a livelihood because of the bounty of nature, but the artisan—shut off from the earth—will be forced by necessity to exercise greater ingenuity in order to secure his means of existence.[67] There will be, therefore, technological innovation as increasing numbers of men turn to industry. Another interesting claim made by Hamilton is that the farmer, with the introduction of labor-saving machinery into industry, will find "a new source of profit and support from the increased industry of his wife and his daughters" as they go to work in the factories.[68] Similarly, he writes of "the employment of persons who would otherwise be idle . . . either from the bias of temper, habit, infirmity of body, or some other cause. . . . It is worthy of particular remark that, in general, women and children are rendered more useful, and the latter more early useful by manufacturing establishments, than they would be otherwise."[69] Where Jefferson looks forward to educating a new generation of children so that they can take their places as citizens, Hamilton cannot wait to enroll them into the labor force "at very tender age."[70] Finally, the extension of machinery, along with the increase in the labor force, will cut down on the owner's cost of "maintaining the labourer."[71] Hamilton foresees all of these advantages in the advancement of industry.

Through the division of labor, technological innovation, the accumulation of capital, and the increased productivity of labor, Hamilton plans to create an American empire, based on capitalism, wherein all levels of society will benefit. Like Locke, commenting on the day laborer in England, Hamilton believes in the trickle-down theory: "It is a truth as important as it is agreeable, and one to which it is not easy to imagine exceptions, that everything tending to establish substantial and permanent order in the affairs of a Country, to increase the total mass of industry and opulence, is ultimately beneficial to every part of it."[72] It is important to remember that it is not for the rich, but by the rich, that America will grow and prosper. Jacob Cooke, a noted Hamiltonian scholar, observes that Hamilton "was more interested in building a prosperous nation by enlisting the aid of the well-to-do than in enriching a class, more concerned with the public good than with private profit." Furthermore, Cooke accurately explains that the public and private sectors are to work together in this enterprise, because Alexander Hamilton rejects the notion of an invisible hand working divine magic.[73] It is imperative, then, for government to encourage industry. "It is important," Hamilton notes, "that the confidence of cautious, sagacious capitalists . . . should be excited. To inspire this description of persons with confidence it is essential that they should be made to see in any project . . . the prospect of such a degree of countenance and support from government as may be capable of overcoming the obstacles, inseparable from first experiments."[74]

The spread of capitalism across the continent, together with the enlargement of the state, sets Hamilton's imagination ablaze with visions of glory. "The industrious habits of the people of the present day absorbed in the pursuit of gain" will create an international order where "a price would be set not only upon our friendship, but upon our neutrality."[75] "Let the thirteen states," he writes, "concur in erecting one great American system superior to the control of all transatlantic force or influence and able to dictate the terms of the connection between the old and the new world!"[76] A fully industrialized United States will become—of this Hamilton is sure—"the admiration and envy of the world."[77]

Hamiltonian economics then, are the negation of Jeffersonian economics. Hamilton longs for empire, opulence, and glory for the nation; whereas Jefferson seeks virtue, freedom, and happiness for the social individual. Jefferson believes that men are sociable, reasonable creatures, who, with the passage of time and the aid of science, can return to the garden. Hamilton, in contrast, views men as "ambitious, vindictive, and rapacious," who, given the opportunity, will turn Jefferson's garden into a pigsty. Between the two philosophic poles in American politics, albeit significantly closer to Hamilton than to Jefferson, nervously stands James Madison. The dispute between Madison and Hamilton, then, was a question of the more prudential means of governing.

Madison, then, must be seen as standing between the two extremes of Jefferson and Hamilton. If each had his dream—Jefferson his pastoralism; Hamilton his capitalism—Madison had his nightmare: willing to pursue neither empire nor Eden, Madison founders about in a sea of despair. His vision is essentially negative. He has no dream. His task is to struggle heroically against the inevitable rise of factions and the growth of capitalism by means of a politicoeconomic system that, by its very nature, made both the rise of factions and the growth of capitalism the preordained result.

To James Madison and to Alexander Hamilton, as to many in America, Jefferson's ideas must have seemed utopian. Throughout his life, whether in France or in Virginia, Jefferson was in exile among his own. Compared to the "realism" of Madison and Hamilton, Jefferson appears to be a naïve, idealistic dreamer. This becomes evident, however, only when Jefferson's philosophy is separated from that of the other Founding Fathers, as well as from the entire mythology surrounding the founding era. After creating the Declaration of Independence and playing a minor role in the Revolutionary War, Jefferson is absent from the American scene. He is not recalled from Europe until the Constitution is a reality; and yet, Americans tend to associate him with the Constitution and with the participants in the Constitutional Convention. The confusion of events in terms of the founding myths is partly understandable, given the obvious attempts of the supporters of the Constitution to invoke the images of the Revolution in order to explain and justify the shift to the right. "There is something decidedly disingenuous about the democratic radicalism of their arguments," writes Gordon Wood. They used "the most popular and democratic rhetoric available to explain and justify their aristocratic system"; they confronted and retarded "the thrust of the Revolution with the rhetoric of the Revolution."[78] Jefferson also helped to initiate and perpetuate this notion of "oneness" by failing clearly and adamantly to sunder himself from the movement.

Nevertheless, when his philosophy is extracted from that of the founding era, it stands out in critical contrast to the

117

American liberalism of Madison and Hamilton. More importantly, it becomes free, once again, to captivate and ignite the American imagination and to offer a legitimate alternative to ''The American Way.''

7

Jefferson's Political Philosophy Revisited: Life, Liberty, and the Pursuit of Happiness

I like the dreams of the future better than the history of the past.[1]

—Jefferson

This reinterpretation of the political philosophy of Thomas Jefferson is almost complete. A return to the introduction is appropriate in attempting to synthesize and evaluate the disjointed parts that constitute the political philosophy of Thomas Jefferson.

Those consensus historians who claim that America always has lacked any legitimate philosophic alternative to its unique brand of market liberalism are in error, for in Jefferson's political ideas can be located a humanist democratic alternative. His unwavering faith in democracy and the ability of humanity to govern itself places him in the radical progressive tradition, looking forward "to the dreams of the future." Using the republican paradigm as a frame of reference, Pocock mistakenly finds a nostalgic Jefferson, a Jefferson who fears modernity. "Jefferson is placing himself, and America," he writes, "at a Rousseauean moment; man can avoid neither becoming civilized nor being corrupted by the process."[2] Jefferson is troubled by the prospects of untamed commercial development; and the canaille of Paris terrify him. But America is not yet commercial, and the citizen-farmer is not the urban rabble. So long as Americans govern themselves, they will rule wisely, provided the necessary education and spirit of revolution are maintained. In the final analysis, it is Jefferson's view of the people—his trust in them—that separates him from others. As he explains it in a letter to his friend Du Pont de

Nemours: "We both consider the people as our children, and love them with parental affection. But you love them as infants whom you are afraid to trust without nurses; and I as adults whom I freely leave to self-government."[3] Since Jefferson did not leave an articulate, systematic account of his political theory, it is understandable how this progressive humanist option has been overlooked. When his political thoughts are woven together, the outline of a radical democratic theory emerges, which presents an alternative not only to the ideologies of the late eighteenth and early nineteenth centuries but also to the American market democracy of the twentieth century and beyond.

The image of the "great collaboration" of Jefferson and Madison continues to haunt the memory of the founding era. Indeed, the term *Jeffersonian* is itself part of this American myth; it has been employed to describe Jefferson and Madison, as well as a host of other persons. "It is notorious," writes Pocock, "that American culture is haunted by myths, many of which arise out of the attempt to escape history and then regenerate it."[4] Insofar as this mythical tradition continues, Jefferson—and all that is associated with his name—continues to provide an ideological cover for the market liberal democracy of the American political system. Plato is correct: Men can love the beautiful. The "traditional" Jefferson continues to provide the legitimizing, "pretty," if not beautiful, drapery with which Americans cover the reality of their possessive individualism. Americans quote the Declaration of Independence, but they live *The Federalist*. Myths die slowly. But once Jefferson's ideas are reexamined, they stand out as alternatives to "the end of classical politics" as embodied in the Constitution.

Although there are some distinct differences between the political theories of Jefferson, Madison, and Hamilton, the disparity between the latter two is in degree, rather than in kind. Hamilton and Madison are firmly in the Anglo-American tradition of possessive individualism. Jefferson is not. That Hamilton hopefully awaited the full development of capitalism, envisioning national wealth, autonomy, power, empire, and glory, whereas Madison anxiously planned to postpone the negative albeit inevitable consequences of that development, makes little difference: both built their theories upon a possessive market society and its possessive individualist concept of man. Within this tradition, a human is seen as an atomistic whole, who "is free and human by virtue of his sole proprietorship of his own person"; moreover, "human society is essentially a series of market relations."[5] Given the structure of a possessive market society, there is inevitably tension between society and the individual. This is not to say, however, that within this concept of humanity the state cannot exercise supreme power over the individual, or that the individual cannot be sacrificed on behalf of the collectivity. While the great mass of humans are blocked from the public arena, the political theories of Hamilton and Madison, like that of Locke, provide for "an individuality that can only fully be realized in accumulating property, and therefore only by some, and only at the expense of the individuality of others. To permit such a society to function, political authority must be supreme over individuals; for if it is not, there can be no assurance that the property institutions essential to this kind of individualism will have adequate sanctions."[6]

Clearly this description of society and individuality fits Hamilton and Madison. Hamilton advocates a powerful national sovereign based on the expansion of capitalism. Once established, this system would spread its largesse to all, becoming the envy of the world. Madison, a reluctant capitalist, lacks the vision to see any way out of the nation's Malthusian fate. To him, the "evil proceeding from" the full market society has to be checked; and yet, government was created to protect men's "diverse faculties" as well as their property. Grudgingly, Madison accepts his *fait accompli*, hoping that his system of government will be able to delay the inevitable decay.

Jefferson, in contrast, is not in the possessive individualist tradition; and the traditional "liberal" interpretations of him are in error. Unlike Hamilton and Madison, Jefferson has a fundamentally different model of humanity. To the authors of *The Federalist*, humans are "ambitious, vindictive, rapacious"; and this was true for "all countries and at all times." Market man becomes universal man. Shays' Rebellion, furthermore, is perceived by both Hamilton and Madison to be all too close to the state of nature. But where they have their market man, Jefferson has the American Indian, who provides the empirical model for his political vision.

Given Jefferson's concept of man, society, and government, it is evident that his political ideas are beyond the liberal "democratic" tradition of his day. Furthermore, his humanism, his communitarian anarchism, and his radical democracy make his political views stand as an alternative to the market liberalism of the past and present.

In regard to humanism, Jefferson holds a fourfold perspective on man and society. One, man is a developing, active, social creature who defines and improves himself through his interaction with nature and other human beings; two, a just society is based on cooperation and human sociability, rather than on competition and human antagonism; three, the economic exploitation and human deprivation created by possessive market society must not be allowed to develop; and four, an egalitarian redistribution—and redefinition—of the social good(s) on an ongoing basis is part of a good society. Jefferson's case for free land, moreover, must be read as being much more than a simple right to property. It is, rather, a specific claim of a right to substantive economic freedom. He realizes that as long as men have the option of finding sustenance on their own farms, they cannot be exploited in the normal forced wage-labor relationship. At minimum, then, Jefferson is arguing for a right *not to be denied* access to the means of labor. But this right is even more significant because Jefferson is really arguing for a right *not to be denied access to the means of life*, not just existence. *Bonheur*, happiness, is man's *telos*. Rights—property and other—are mere instruments to aid men in their pursuit of happiness. And governments must either be structured or dissolved and restructured so that all men will have access to this pursuit.[7]

Jefferson argues that man is an active, developing, innately moral creature. He is a social being. Living with other humans in harmonious small rural communities is part of a fully human life. In such an environment, virtue, intimacy, and humanity can flourish. Occasionally led astray from what is moral, the unguided intellect can be a problem, but more often than not, the environmental factors of overcrowded cities, bleak working conditions, the absence of economic freedom, and the presence of economic exploitation are what cause the lapse in social behavior. Consequently, Jefferson argues for a distinctly noncapitalistic economic system, in which every man will always have the option of sustaining and nurturing himself and his family on a small farm. This pastoral life style is based, not on profit, but on science, moderation, and beauty: Jefferson wants the optimum return on energy exerted so that "leisure" and a time "to think" will be available at the end of the day. In many ways, Jefferson's own life exemplifies the ideal of the civic-humanist tradition. Although he did not consider himself to be the intellectual equal of a Franklin or a Rittenhouse, Jefferson was a most versatile person. Anthropology, philology, politics, law, classics, belles-lettres, philosophy, architecture, farming, and nail making were but some of the activities in which he engaged. According to the civic-humanist tradition, man's essence, Pocock appropriately notes, is not only the "Aristotelian citizen" but also the "undistracted, unspecialised man—hunter in the morning and critic in the afternoon" whom Marx described in *The German Ideology* and "hoped to restore to his universality."[8] To allow this humanity to develop, advances in all sciences, political as well as mechanical and agricultural, are needed. Although advances in science and technology are advantageous, moderation in material desires is also essential. Jefferson sees the dual possibilities of splendor and decadence. The market side of man is what causes Jefferson the gravest concern, for if men forget "themselves" but "in the sole faculty of making money," the result will be their "eating one another," as in Europe. To Jefferson, commodities and profit are always of secondary interest. His good life consists of friendship, felicity, and freedom. The last of these necessitates ward-republics, permanent revolution, and free land.

In regard to communitarian anarchism, Jefferson's repeated use of the American Indian as an edifying countercultural example of how men can live in a community without the need for formal government is demonstrative of his anarchist tendency. Scientistlike, Jefferson carefully studied these men and their society. From his empirical observations he draws a picture of life among these men similar to Rousseau's fictional account of the Golden Age in his *Second Discourse*. Knowing that the Indians appear to be alive and happy in their simple society, Jefferson believes that technology and scientific farming could set them free from the domination of nature. This places Jefferson apart from Rousseau, who wants to hold scientific development to a minimum, often viewing it as the sorcerer's apprentice. In a telling passage of his *Second Discourse*, Rousseau metaphorically captures what he sees as the hidden costs to the arts and sciences. After describing the development first of vanity and then of property, he laments the result: "vast forests were changed into smiling fields which had to be watered with the sweat of men, and in which slavery and misery were soon seen to germinate and grow with the crops." Rousseau further explains that "metallurgy and agriculture" are what have produced this "great revolution"; put another way, "it is iron and wheat which civilized men and ruined the human race."[9] Small wonder that Rousseau fears modernity; Jefferson, however, looks ahead. He is captivated by "metallurgy and agriculture," eagerly awaiting their further development. In the Baconian tradition, Jefferson naïvely believes that science can do no wrong. With the addition of scientific farming, then, the Indians will have, in their own way, all that Jefferson longs for.

For Jefferson, as for Herbert Marcuse, anthropologic evidence of harmonious communities without governments serves two purposes: it raises serious challenges to the

Madison-Hamilton view of market man as universal man; and it offers a kind of metaphoric ideal for the type of communal life—without regressing backward historically in terms of science, technology, and enlightenment—towards which modern humans ought to aspire.

The Arcadian age is past. A return to a republic of small, virtuous farms appears to be infeasible. This Jefferson knows. Consquently, this aspect of Jefferson must also be read in terms of its intention. His pastoralism is based on a conception of the golden mean. Even in his most vehement diatribes against city life, Jeffeson never argues either for the wilderness or for hunting-and-gathering tribes. He wants a modicum of civilization—that is, he wants rational science to be blended with the wilds to produce a beautiful, well-groomed, and bountiful garden. Perhaps Leo Marx explains Jefferson's pastoralism best: "The controlling principle of Jefferson's politics is not to be found in any fixed image of society. Rather it is dialectical. It lies in his recognition of the constant need to redefine the 'middle landscape' ideal, pushing it ahead, so to speak, into an unknown future to adjust it to ever-changing circumstances. (The ideal, in fact, is an abstract embodiment of the concept of mediation between the extremes of primitivism and what may be called 'over-civilization.')"[10] There is, then, this aesthetic side to Jefferson. Pastoralism's golden mean presents a healthy, beautiful environment in which men can grow and develop.

Nevertheless, the possessive market society continues to grow ad infinitum; vampirelike, it sucks the earth and its inhabitants of life. In such an environment, moderation is considered to be illiberal. Men define themselves in terms of what and whom they own. By bringing this aesthetic dimension back into the American ethos, a sense of order, harmony, and limits would result. When citizens are not forced to be at each other's throats by an economic system, innate sociability and communal interaction could thrive.

With regard to radical democracy, Jefferson was America's first and foremost advocate of permanent revolution. Revolution helps to keep both humanity and society healthy,

125

happy, and alive. It is, moreover, part of his idea of the good life, from which no one should be denied access.

Jefferson's political system specifically calls for mass participatory democracy. He advocates a pyramid structure of government in which each higher level is held directly and immediately accountable to its next lower level. Politics, furthermore, is to become a daily part of human life; no longer will it be a biennial, momentary fulfillment of a duty. Like Rousseau's conception of morality in *The Social Contract*, upon which Kant, Hegel, and the German Idealist tradition erected itself, Jefferson also considers obedience to self-prescribed laws to be the only appropriate conception of freedom. Participation ensures this; it is also a constant check against tyranny and an additional avenue in which men can pursue happiness. Freedom also requires that each generation must have the chance to begin society over again; every twenty years, all the laws would automatically become void. Laws are not "sanctimonious"; they have to be rewritten to suit the change in circumstances as well as men. Recognizing the need for every generation to begin anew, Jefferson's open-ended political philosophy actively encourages individuals, within the guidelines of political participation, economic freedom, and moral responsibility, to create and re-create community. These celebrations of democratic community, moreover, simultaneously provide a good opportunity to redistribute property, thereby protecting an individual's economic independence. They also keep the society in a state of constant revolution, in harmony with human and social evolution. Participatory democracy in both the political realm and the economic realm is, to Jefferson, a necessary prerequisite to human fulfillment.

To state that Jefferson holds any teleological position, then, must be properly understood. Men must be allowed to make their own history consciously. But this history and the manner of creating it are themselves subject to human alteration. It is the right to create, rather than the creation itself, that must be valued above all. As a contemporary democrat has put it, "It is better to travel than to arrive."[11]

Notes

Chapter 1
The "Jeffersonian" Tradition: The Future of an Illusion

1. Thomas Jefferson (hereafter cited as TJ) to Charles Thomson, 20 Sept. 1787, *The Works of Thomas Jefferson*, ed. Paul Leicester Ford, 12 vols. (New York: Knickerbocker Press, 1904), 5:342 (hereafter cited as *Works of TJ*).

2. In 1943 the noted historian Douglass Adair remarked that it takes "considerable courage" for anyone to try to write anything original about Thomas Jefferson. Still, Adair felt compelled to pursue his own Jefferson interest, believing that a "re-analysis" was justified because it would enable a more encompassing interpretation to surface. It is in this spirit that the present effort is made. See Douglass Greybill Adair, "The Intellectual Origins of Jeffersonian Democracy: Republicanism, the Class Struggle, and the Virtuous Farmer" (Ph.D. diss., Yale University, 1943).

3. To a considerable extent the problematic nature in the divergent interpretations of Jefferson is understandable. Although he was a prolific writer, with the notable exception of the classic but brief *Notes on the State of Virginia*, Jefferson left posterity neither a systematic nor an extended account of his political ideas. The theoretician, consequently, is forced to sift through volumes of seemingly unrelated letters, speeches, memoranda, articles, and other fragmentary communications; then, some order must be imposed on this plethora of material. Julian P. Boyd, editor of *The Papers of Thomas Jefferson*, 20 vols. (Princeton, N.J.: Princeton University Press, 1950–82; hereafter cited as *Papers of TJ*), estimates the number of Jefferson correspondences to be upwards of fifty thousand separate items. In a sense, it is necessary for the Jeffersonian scholar to adopt the style of an astronomer who, standing before the infinity of space, tries to comprehend and, as parsimoniously as possible, to explain the heavenly order behind the countless visual stimuli, assuming that there is an order to be imposed.

An additional difficulty to reaching an understanding of Jefferson is the fact that he was also a public man. He spent much of his adult life in the realm of the "obviously political": governor of Virginia, minister to France, secretary of state, vice-president, and president were but some of the political positions he held. And as several recent studies of slavery have shown, Jefferson's practice often lagged behind his theory. Still, this work is an examination of Jefferson's political ideas. The public facet to the man, although not ignored, will be given secondary consideration. The point here is that the amount of weight that any interpretation places on Jefferson's public life will influence the Jefferson discovered. Both the state of his writings and the style of his life, then, present formidable obstacles to Jeffersonian scholarship and help to explain the voluminous explorations and divergent interpretations of him.

4. Bernard Bailyn, *The Origins of American Politics* (New York: Alfred A. Knopf, 1970), pp. 3-10. Bailyn identifies five schools of interpretation.

5. Charles A. Beard, *An Economic Interpretation of the Constitution of the United States* (New York: Macmillan Co., 1913, 1935); and in *Economic Origins of Jeffersonian Democracy* (New York: Macmillan Co., 1915), his opening epigraph is a direct quotation from Turner: "We may trace the contest between the capitalist and the democratic pioneer from the earliest colonial days" (*American Historical Review*, 16:227).

6. Beard, *Economic Interpretation*, pp. viii, xvi, x.

7. Ibid., p. 324.

8. At least two things must be noted about Beard's presentation. First, while the United States was embroiled in the Second World War, Beard substantially changed both the tenor and the content of his conflict thesis. He altered his position both on the Founding Fathers and on the nature of the conflict in general. In *The Republic: Conversations on Fundamentals* (New York: Viking Press, 1943), Beard observes that one of the general interpretations of American history views it as "the outcome of a conflict between radical or agrarian forces on the one side and the forces of conservative or capitalistic reaction on the other." After he admits that a conflict is indeed taking place, he then shifts ground on the number of parties involved, as well as on their ideological position: a third party, "an influential group on the extreme right of the conservatives," must now be incorporated into his thesis (p. 24). This addition to Beard's earlier work, as Richard Hofstadter has pointed out, had "the effect of pushing the founding fathers from the far right into the center of the political spectrum, . . . making the adoption of The Constitution much less a victory of capitalism . . . over agrarianism" (*The Progressive Historians: Turner, Beard, Parrington* [New York: Alfred A. Knopf, 1968], p. 221). Second, while Beard's general conflict position changes with the times, his treatment of Jefferson, which never tries to comprehend his political theory in its entirety, is continually reductive and flawed. In *An Economic Interpretation* he does not discuss Jefferson; even in *Economic Origins of Jeffersonian Democracy* Beard does not offer an analysis of Jefferson's

political theory. Instead, as in *An Economic Interpretation*, he traces the sociopolitical background of the members of the Constitutional Convention, extending the list to other notable Americans not present at Philadelphia, e.g., John Adams and Thomas Jefferson. Once more he concludes that "it is established upon a statistical basis that the Constitution of the United States was the product of a conflict between capitalistic and agrarian interests" (p. 464). Given Jefferson's class orientation and Beard's method, Beard is forced to maintain that "Jeffersonian Democracy simply meant the possession of the federal government by the agrarian masses led by the aristocracy of slave-owning planters, and the theoretical repudiation of the right to use Government for the benefit of any capitalistic groups, fiscal, banking, or manufacturing" (p. 467).

Critiques of Beard's works are numerous, and this analysis need not add to the weighty indictment. On the basis of the interpretation that follows, Beard's hasty conclusion of what Jeffersonian Democracy "simply meant" will be shown to be erroneous.

9. Hofstadter claims that Parrington is now rarely read, except to refute him (*Progressive Historians*), p. 349.

10. Vernon Louis Parrington (*Main Currents of American Thought: American Literature from the Beginning to 1920*, 3 vols. [New York: Harcourt, Brace, & Co., Inc., 1927-30], p. iii) claims to "have chosen to follow the broad path of our political, economic, and social development, rather than the narrower belletristic."

11. Ibid., p. vi.

12. Ibid., p. v.

13. Parrington's treatment of political theory is, at best, spotty. He understands neither the physiocrats nor Luther; and he mistakenly thinks that Rousseau's influence can explicitly be found in many places during the colonial period. Like Beard's, his work has been subject to scathing critiques; like Beard, he does not attempt a systematic treatment of the political thought of any of the founders: Hamilton, Adams, and Jefferson each receives a short, overly simplified analysis; and James Madison, a figure of no small import in American history, receives but a solitary paragraph. Parrington, then, offers little beyond clichés and generalizations to the study of Jefferson.

14. Daniel Bell, *The End of Ideology: On the Exhaustion of Political Ideas in the Fifties* (Glencoe, Ill.: Free Press, 1960).

15. Daniel Boorstin, *The Genius of American Politics* (Chicago: University of Chicago Press, 1953), passim; and Louis Hartz, *The Liberal Tradition in America: An Interpretation of American Thought since the Revolution* (New York: Harcourt, Brace, & Co., 1955), pp. 3–86; and *The Founding of New Societies: Studies in the History of the United States, Latin America, South Africa, Canada, and Australia* (New York: Harcourt, Brace, & World, Inc., 1964), pp. 3–23.

16. Alexis de Tocqueville, *Democracy in America*, 2 vols. (New York:

Schocken Books, 1961). See *Henry Adams: The Education of Henry Adams*, ed. Edward N. Saveth (New York: Washington Square Press, Inc., 1963), pp. 38–209, where Adams points out the vast differences in the sociopolitical make-up in the United States in 1800 compared to 1817. Although Jefferson spanned both periods, Tocqueville's description is that of the post-1817 era, when America had already begun to move rapidly out of Jefferson's pastoral vision.

17. Boorstin, *Genius*. He hardly tries to hide the obvious political motives of his work. This tendency, more often than not, makes it difficult to treat his ideas seriously.

18. Ibid., p. 8.

19. Ibid., p. 1.

20. Ibid., p. 170.

21. Ibid., p. 161.

22. Ibid., p. 162; this passage is symbolic of the style of the language, with its quasi-religious overtones, that Boorstin uses throughout.

23. Hartz, *Founding of New Societies*, p. 3.

24. Hartz, *Liberal Tradition*, p. 20.

25. Louis Hartz, "The Rise of the Democratic Idea," in *Paths of American Thought*, ed. Arthur M. Schlesinger, Jr., and Morton White (London: Chatto & Windus, 1964), p. 44.

26. Ibid., p. 46.

27. Hartz, *Liberal Tradition*, p. 5.

28. Hartz, "Rise," p. 47.

29. Hartz, *Liberal Tradition*, p. 140. As a general interpretation of American history, Hartz's theory is brilliant. Painted in broad brush strokes, it is difficult to fault. However, when Hartz focuses on Jefferson, some difficulties arise.

Hartz discusses a certain "European flavor" to Jefferson's thought, which places Jefferson, along with Franklin, outside the mainstream of American political theory. It is difficult to know exactly what Hartz means by this. True, both Jefferson and Franklin spent considerable time on the Continent and were impressed, and likely influenced, by philosophic thought there. But if Hartz is suggesting that the two theorists are similar in their political theory, he is greatly mistaken: the author of *Notes on the State of Virginia* could serve only as the anti-hero of Max Weber's *The Protestant Ethic and the Spirit of Capitalism*. Still, Hartz's observation that Jefferson was never the spokesperson for the dominant trend in American politics is accurate.

At least one additional problem with Hartz's Jefferson must be pointed out. Wishing to demonstrate the uniqueness of the American experience, in his *Liberal Tradition* Hartz compares Jefferson to Disraeli. The two, Hartz claims, agree on many points: the countryside can cultivate virtue as well as food; the cities, decadence as well as commerce. Yet, the differences between Disraeli and Jefferson illustrate the peculiarity of European thought when transferred to the New World. "Disraeli sees the land as fostering an ancient feudal order and the towns as fostering democracy, while Jefferson sees the land as fostering democracy and the towns a quasi-feudal kind of social dependence'' (p. 120). Hartz concludes this brief juxtaposition with the observation that ''a Disraeli was a world apart from a Jefferson: the one had the feudal spirit, the other had the spirit of the small liberal enterpreneur'' (p. 125). On this point, Hartz is mistaken, again. Jefferson advocated the small farm, but not merely as a liberal entrepreneurial enterprise. It is, rather, both the organic nature of the farm community, which is reminiscent of feudalism, and the freedom from coercion provided by free land, which he wants to transfer to society at large. Cities, moreover, are not seen by Jefferson as quasi-feudal, even though they can be the source of social decay. As will become clear, then, Hartz's portrait of Jefferson reflects the real Jefferson but dimly.

30. Bernard Bailyn, ed., *Pamphlets of the American Revolution, 1750–1776* (Cambridge: Belknap Press of Harvard University Press, 1965), *The Ideological Origins of the American Revolution* (Cambridge: Belknap Press of Harvard University Press, 1967), and *The Origins of American Politics* (New York: Alfred A. Knopf, 1970); Gordon S. Wood, *The Creation of the American Republic, 1776–1787* (Chapel Hill: Published for the Institute of Early American History and Culture at Williamsburg, Virginia, by the University of North Carolina Press, 1969); J. G. A. Pocock, *The Machiavellian Moment: Florentine Political Thought and the Atlantic Republican Tradition* (Princeton, N.J.: Princeton University Press, 1975). The term ''Neo-Whig'' is not mine, but is borrowed from a growing body of literature on this debate between ideas (and which paradigm of ideas) and economics. Several excellent analyses of the historiography of the founding have already been published, thus eliminating the necessity to duplicate the effort here. See Robert E. Shalhope, ''Republicanism and Early American Historiography,'' *William and Mary Quarterly* 39 (Apr. 1982): 334–56; and his ''Toward a Republican Synthesis: The Emergence of an Understanding of Republicanism in American Historiography,'' *William and Mary Quarterly* 29, no. 1 (Jan. 1972): 49–80; John M. Murrin, ''The Great Inversion, or Court versus Country: A Comparison of the Revolution Settlements in England (1688–1721) and America (1776–1816),'' in *Three British Revolutions: 1641, 1688, 1776*, ed. J. G. A. Pocock (Princeton, N.J.: Princeton University Press, 1980), pp. 368–453; Isaac Kramnick, ''Republican Revisionism Revisited,'' *American Historical Review* 87, no. 3 (June 1982): 629–64; Joyce Appleby, ''The Social Origins of American Revolutionary Ideology,'' *Journal of American History* 64 (Mar. 1978): 935–58; and Daniel Walker Howe, ''European Sources of Political Ideas in Jeffersonian America,'' *Reviews in American History*, Dec. 1982, pp. 28–44.

31. Shalhope, ''Republicanism,'' p. 335.

32. The best treatment of this time is Isaac Kramnick's *Bolingbroke and His Circle: The Politics of Nostalgia in the Age of Walpole* (Cambridge: Harvard University Press, 1968).

33. Bernard Bailyn, ''The Central Themes of the American Revolution:

An Interpretation,'' in *Essays on the American Revolution,* ed. Stephen G. Kurtz and James H. Hutson (Chapel Hill and New York: Published for the Institute of Early American History and Culture, Williamsburg, Virginia, by the University of North Carolina Press, and W. W. Norton & Co., Inc., 1973), pp. 12–13.

34. Wood, *Creation,* pp. 606–7; see also p. 562. Cf. Richard Buel, Jr., *Securing the Revolution: Ideology in American Politics, 1789–1815* (Ithaca, N.Y.: Cornell University Press, 1972). Buel confirms the presence of the ideological debate during the Federalist-Republican debates, but he does not attempt to locate the origin of the ideas.

35. Pocock, *Machiavellian Moment,* pp. 527, 546, vii, viii.

36. See Murrin, "Great Inversion," p. 373; and Shalhope, "Republicanism," p. 337, especially n. 9.

37. Kramnick, "Republican Revisionism," p. 655; see also Joyce Appleby, "Social Origins," p. 937, who correctly claims that "there is more at stake than historiography in these conflicting interpretations of the ideological origins of the American Revolution. If a classical republicanism imbued with traditional notions of political authority dominated colonial thinking, where are the roots of that liberalism which flowered so quickly after independence? Having eschewed intellectual history for the study of consciousness, the Neo-Whigs have unavoidably provoked curiosity about the relation of ideas to the social context in which they were held. Does a premodern revolutionary ideology argue for a premodern colonial society as well? If the Revolution was fought in a frenzy over corruption, out of fear of tyranny, and with hopes for redemption through civic virtue, where and when are scholars to find the sources for the aggressive individualism, the optimistic materialism, and the pragmatic interest-group politics that became so salient so early in the life of the new nation?''

38. Murrin compares the scholarly interaction to the children's hand-symbol game of scissors, paper, rock; each individual in the game, moreover, seems to be compelled to pledge unwavering alliances to one school or the other. See his "Great Inversion," pp. 374–75.

39. Carl L. Becker, *The Declaration of Independence: A Study in the History of Political Ideas* (New York: Random House, 1958), pp. 27, 79.

40. See Howe, "European Sources," pp. 30–33.

41. Judith Shklar, "Inventing America: Jefferson's Declaration of Independence by Garry Wills," *New Republic,* 26 Aug. and 2 Sept. 1978 p. 32. See also Kenneth S. Lynn, "The Regressive Historians," *American Scholar* 47, no. 4 (Autumn 1978): 471–500; and Ronald Hamowy, "Jefferson and the Scottish Enlightenment: A Critique of Garry Wills's *Inventing America: Jefferson's Declaration of Independence,*" *William and Mary Quarterly* 36, no. 4 (Oct. 1979): 503.

42. Paul Merrill Spurlin, *Rousseau in America: 1760–1809* (University: University of Alabama Press, 1969), p. 113.

43. Pocock, *Machiavellian Moment,* pp. 533, 541, 545–46.

44. Forrest McDonald, *The Presidency of Thomas Jefferson* (Lawrence: University Press of Kansas, 1976), pp. ix, 19.

45. Drew R. McCoy, *The Elusive Republic: Political Economy in Jeffersonian America* (Chapel Hill: Published for the Institute of Early American History and Culture, Williamsburg, Virginia, by the University of North Carolina Press, 1980), pp. 9–10.

46. Pocock, *Machiavellian Moment*, pp. 546, 541.

47. In her *Capitalism and a New Social Order: The Republican Vision of the 1790s* (New York and London: New York University Press, 1983), p. 79, Appleby suggests that the vision of the future is an "effective litmus test" for differentiating the Jeffersonians from the Federalists. It is also an effective test for separating Jefferson out from the civic-humanist tradition.

48. See Joyce Appleby, "What Is Still American in the Political Philosophy of Thomas Jefferson?" *William and Mary Quarterly* 39 (Apr. 1982): 291, 293, 295–96; and her "Social Origins," p. 955.

49. See Kramnick, "Republican Revisionism," p. 645, where he quotes a yet-unpublished piece by Appleby, where she apparently states that "what was distinctive about the Republican's economic policy was not an anticommercial bias, but a commitment to growth through the unimpeded exertions of individuals" with "access to economic opportunity." Although not specifically discussing Jefferson, Kramnick appears to be sympathetic to Appleby's Jefferson (see pp. 662–64). While both are correct that a shift occurs in liberalism from the public to the private, Jefferson's position is closer to the classical model than they think.

50. Richard Hofstadter, *The Age of Reform: From Bryan to F.D.R.* (New York: Alfred A. Knopf, 1955), pp. 3–59.

51. Joyce Appleby, "Commercial Farming and the 'Agrarian Myth' in the Early Republic," *Journal of American History* 68 (Mar. 1982): 834–38.

52. Ibid., pp. 844–45.

53. Ibid., p. 849.

54. Appleby, *Capitalism*, pp. 22–23.

55. H. Mark Roelofs, *Ideology and Myth in American Politics* (Boston: Little, Brown & Co., 1976), p. 247.

56. Max J. Skidmore, *American Political Thought* (New York: St. Martin's Press, 1978), pp. 70, 72–73.

57. Among those in addition to the above who also hold to this tradition are Merrill D. Peterson, *Thomas Jefferson and the New Nation: A Biography* (New York: Oxford University Press, 1970); Richard Hofstadter, *The American Political Tradition and the Men Who Made It* (New York: Random House, 1973); Dumas Malone, *Jefferson and His Time*, 6 vols. (Boston: Little, Brown & Co., 1948–81); Julian Boyd, *The Declaration of Independence: The Evolution of the Text* (Princeton, N.J.: Princeton University Press, 1945); and Charles Maurice Wiltse, *The Jeffersonian Tradition in American Democracy* (Chapel Hill: University of North Carolina Press, 1935).

58. Hannah Arendt, *On Revolution* (New York: Viking Press, 1963), pp. 217–85.

59. Leo Marx, *The Machine in the Garden: Technology and the Pastoral Ideal in America* (New York: Oxford University Press, 1964), pp. 73–144. Throughout this study I use the term "pastoral" in Leo Marx's sense, rather than in the sense of the political economists who equate pastoral with herding. See chapter 3 for a more detailed account.

60. C. B. Macpherson, *Democratic Theory: Essays in Retrieval* (Oxford: Clarendon Press, 1973), pp. 135–36; and, *The Life and Times of Liberal Democracy* (New York: Oxford University Press, 1977), pp. 17–23.

61. Garry Wills, *Inventing America: Jefferson's Declaration of Independence* (Garden City, N.Y.: Doubleday & Co., 1978), passim.

62. Sheldon S. Wolin, *Politics and Visions: Continuity and Innovation in Western Political Thought* (Boston: Little, Brown & Co., 1960), p. 297. See also the excellent study of Jefferson's radicalism contained in Staughton Lynd, *Intellectual Origins of American Radicalism* (New York: Pantheon Books, 1968), pp. 3–100.

Chapter 2
Property: "The Earth Belongs to the Living"

1. TJ to James Madison, 6 Sept. 1789, *Papers of TJ*, 15:392. To Major John Cartwright, 15 June 1824, Jefferson writes: "But can they [constitutions] be made unchangeable? Can one generation bind another, and all others, in succession forever? I think not. The Creator has made the earth for the living, not the dead. Rights and powers can only belong to persons, not to things, not to mere matter, unendowed with will. The dead are not even things. The particles of matter which composed their bodies, make part now of the bodies of other animals, vegetables, or minerals of a thousand forms. To what then are attached the rights and powers they held while in form of men? A generation may bind itself as long as its majority continues in life; when that has disappeared, another majority is in place, holds all the rights and powers their predecessors once held, and may change their laws and institutions to suit themselves. Nothing then is unchangeable but the inherent and unalienable rights of man" (*The Writings of Thomas Jefferson*, ed. H. A. Washington, 9 vols. [Washington, D.C.: Taylor & Maury, 1854], 7:359; hereafter cited as *Writings of TJ* [Washington]). Adrienne Koch, in *Jefferson and Madison: The Great Collaboration* (New York: Oxford University Press, 1976), verifies Jefferson's claim of originality. She argues that Thomas Paine got the idea of "the earth belongs to the living" from Jefferson (see pp. 81–91).

2. TJ to James Madison, 6 Sept. 1789, *Papers of TJ*, 15:392.

3. Cf. Morton White, *The Philosophy of the American Revolution* (New York: Oxford University Press, 1978), pp. 15–96. White presents a lengthy argument, attempting to show that John Locke drew a distinction between "innate" and "self-evident" principles. The former, Locke refutes; the latter, he defends. Rather than enter into this debate, White's argument

assumes that Locke and Burlamaqui are "the source" of Jefferson's ideas. This approach is problematic. At no time, so far as I am aware, does Jefferson claim Locke—or any other philosopher—as his guiding political theorist. Instead of attempting to determine who influenced Jefferson on this point, it is more fruitful to take Jefferson at his word—namely, that all men have a "moral sense" and that it is specifically this sense which makes men gregarious. For a contrasting position to White's, see Wiltse, *Jeffersonian Tradition*, pp. 67–72.

4. TJ to James Madison, 6 Sept. 1789, *Papers of TJ*, 15:392–93.

5. Ibid., p. 393. Note also the ecological implication of this passage. Similar statements are found throughout Jefferson's writings; this ecological ethic, discussed later, complements the nonmarket mentality of Jefferson's politics.

6. Ibid., p. 396.

7. Ibid.

8. On other occasions, Jefferson calculated the time at every thirty-four years. The exact number of years is unimportant; the intent of the principle is the paramount fact to be remembered.

9. See TJ to Roger O. Weightman, 24 June 1826, *Works of TJ*, 12:477, with regard to the first point. "All eyes are opened, or opening, to the rights of man. The general spread of the light of science has already laid open to every view the palpable truth, that the mass of mankind has not been born with saddles on their backs, now a favored few booted and spurred, ready to ride them legitimately, by the grace of God."

10. TJ to Samuel Kercheval, 12 July 1816, *Works of TJ*, 12:12.

11. TJ to James Madison, 6 Sept. 1789, *Papers of TJ*, 15:395–96.

12. For a discussion of this concept as elaborated by TJ, see Koch, *Jefferson and Madison*, pp. 62–96. TJ's continuing adherence is reflected in letters to John Eppes, 24 June 1813; to Samuel Kercheval, 12 July 1816, *Works of TJ*, 12:12; to William Plumer, 21 July 1816; and to Thomas Earle, 23 Sept. 1823.

13. James Madison to TJ, 4 Feb. 1790, *Papers of TJ*, 16:151, 154.

14. See "Federalist No. 10," *The Federalist*, ed. Jacob E. Cooke (Middletown, Conn.: Wesleyan University Press, 1982), pp. 56–65 (hereafter cited as *Federalist*).

15. Cf. Koch, *Jefferson and Madison*, passim. As the title suggests, Koch prefers to emphasize those elements which the two men held in common; hence, her interpretation is the archetype of most of the Jefferson literature.

16. "A Summary View of the Rights of British Americans," July 1774, *Papers of TJ*, 1:122.

17. Ibid., pp. 122, 123.

18. Ibid., p. 133; see also William Blackstone, *Commentaries on the Laws of England*, vol. 2 (Oxford: Clarendon Press, 1765), pp. 1–162.

19. Joyotpaul Chaudhuri, "Possession, Ownership and Access: A Jeffersonian View of Property," *Political Inquiry* 1, no. 1 (Fall 1973): 78–95.

20. "The Declaration of Independence as Adopted by Congress," *Papers of TJ*, 1:429. To M. Coray, 31 Oct. 1923, he writes: "The equal rights of man and the happiness of every individual, are now acknowledged to be the only legitimate objects of government" (*Writings of TJ*, 7:319).

21. Koch, *Jefferson and Madison*, p. 80.

22. Since life, liberty, and happiness were natural rights and since property was but a civil right, Jefferson had little sympathy for slave owners who complained about stealing by slaves. See *Notes on the State of Virginia*, ed. William Peden (New York: W. W. Norton, 1972), p. 142; hereafter cited as *Notes on Virginia*. See TJ to Edward Bancroft, 26 Jan. 1788, *Papers of TJ*, 14:492–94.

23. See "Bill to Enable Tenants in Fee Tail to Convey Their Lands in Fee Simple," *Papers of TJ*, 1:560–62; "Autobiography," 1821, *Works of TJ*, 1:58, 77–78; "Services of Jefferson," 1800?, *Works of TJ*, 9:163–66.

24. TJ to the Reverend James Madison, 28 Oct. 1785, *Papers of TJ*, 8:681–82.

25. Wiltse, *Jeffersonian Tradition*, p. 138; and Lynd argues (*Intellectual Origins*, p. 83) that Jefferson "seemed to imply that, in the absence of remedial state action, the unemployed might rightly take the land they needed." For a contrasting interpretation of Locke see James Tully, *A Discourse on Property: John Locke and His Adversaries* (Cambridge: Cambridge University Press, 1980).

26. See Koch, *Jefferson and Madison*, p. 78; Wiltse, *Jeffersonian Tradition*, p. 74; Wills, *Inventing America*, p. 249; and Gilbert Chinard, ed., *The Correspondence of Jefferson and Dupont de Nemours* (Baltimore, Md.: Johns Hopkins Press, 1931), pp. lxii–lxiii.

27. Koch, *Jefferson and Madison*, p. 79; on pp. 92–96 Koch notes some difficulties that this idea would present for capitalist economic development but claims that pragmatism forced Jefferson to abandon a literal interpretaton of his doctrine.

28. Lynd, *Intellectual Origins*, pp. 77, 8, and passim.

Chapter 3
Political Economy: Land, Liberty, and Leisure

1. TJ to Geismar, 6 Sept. 1785, *Papers of TJ*, 8:500.

2. C. B. Macpherson, *Political Theory of Possessive Individualism: Hobbes to Locke* (Oxford: Clarendon Press, 1962), pp. 1–68, 263–78.

3. TJ to John Adams, 28 Oct. 1813, *The Adams-Jefferson Letters*, ed. Lester J. Cappon (New York: Simon & Schuster, 1971), p. 391; hereafter cited as *A-J Letters*. This passage also shows that Jefferson clearly saw what Macpherson calls the net transfer of power. See Macpherson, *Life and Times of Liberal Democracy*, p. 18; see also his *Political Theory*, pp. 46–61, where he carefully delineates three models of society that serve as useful

analytical tools to help understand the crucial politicoeconomic differences among theorists. Macpherson's "Simple Market Society" accurately reflects the basic properties of Jefferson's ideal society: "(a) There is no authoritative allocation of work: individuals are free to expend their energies, skills, and goods as they will. (b) There is no authoritative provision of rewards for work: individuals are not given or guaranteed, by the state or community, rewards appropriate to their social functions. (c) There is authoritative definition and enforcement of contracts. (d) All individuals seek rationally to maximize their utilities, that is, to get the most satisfaction they can for a given expenditure of energy or goods, or to get a given satisfaction for the least possible expenditure of energy or goods. (e) All individuals have land or other resources on which they may get a living by their labour." In order to "absolutely" rule out the evolution of this "Simple Market Society" into a "Possessive Market Society," Macpherson adds an additional postulate: "(f) That the satisfaction of retaining control of one's own labour is greater than the difference between expected wages and expected returns as an independent producer." Although this postulate would be embraced by Jefferson as being "self-evident," he is quite willing to allow men to enter into wage-labor contracts because postulate (e), which in Jefferson amounts to fifty acres of land, helps to ensure that the contract will not be exploitive. Free land, then, becomes the guarantor of economic and political freedom.

4. William M. Van der Weyde, ed., *The Life and Works of Thomas Paine,* 10 vols., Patriots' ed. (New Rochelle, N.Y.: Thomas Paine National Historical Association, 1925). *Agrarian Justice* is in vol. 10, pp. 1–38; see p. 30.

5. Ibid., pp. 11–12.

6. Ibid., p. 15.

7. TJ to Thomas Digges, 19 June 1788, *Papers of TJ,* 13:260.

8. This terminology is adopted from the works of C. B. Macpherson, supra.

9. "The Virginia Constitution," *Papers of TJ,* 1:329–86. The sole difference in the three drafts on this point is that in the final version the grant was placed in a separate section titled "Rights, Public and Private." As governor of Virginia during the Revolutionary War, Jefferson issued a proclamation granting fifty acres of land to anyone who would desert from the British Armies (see *Papers of TJ,* 4:505). It is interesting to note that Richard Hofstadter, in *The American Political Tradition,* p. 39, fails to see the obvious connection. In the body of his text, Hofstadter claims that Jefferson never tried to introduce universal suffrage for white males. Then, in a footnote, he remarks that Jefferson proposed a grant of land to all white males, which "would have made suffrage practically universal."

10. Adair ("Intellectual Origin," p. 10) points out that *economy,* in the eighteenth century, was a political term as well as an economic one.

11. *Notes on Virginia,* p. 161.

12. TJ to Thomas Pleasants, 8 May 1786, *Papers of TJ,* 9:472–73.

13. TJ to Nathaniel Tracy, 17 Aug. 1785, *Papers of TJ*, 8:399.

14. TJ to Archibald Stuart, 25 Jan. 1786, *Papers of TJ*, 9:218. Consider also Jefferson's remark to James Currie, 4 Aug. 1787, *Papers of TJ*, 11:682: "How happy a people were we during the War from the single circumstance that we could not run in debt. This counteracted all the inconveniences we felt, as the present facility of ruining ourselves overweighs all the blessings of peace. I know no condition happier than that of a Virginia farmer might be, conducting himself as he did during the war. His estate supplies a good table, clothes itself and his family with their ordinary apparel, furnishes a small surplus to buy salt, sugar, coffee, and a little finery for his wife and daughter, enables him to receive and to visit his friends, and furnishes him pleasing and healthy occupation. To secure all this he needs but one act of self denial, to put off buying anything till he has money to pay for it."

15. TJ to Samuel Kercheval, 12 July 1816, *Works of TJ*, 12:10. This sentiment appears many times in his writings. Another notable example is this passage: "New schemes are on foot for bringing more paper to market by encouraging great manufacturing companies to form, and their actions, or paper-shares, to be transferable as bank-stock. We are ruined, Sir, if we do not over rule the principles that 'the more we owe, the more prosperous we shall be,' 'that a public debt furnishes the means of enterprise,' 'that if ours should be once paid off, we should incur another by any means however extravagant' &c. &c." (TJ to James Monroe, 17 Apr. 1791, *Works of TJ*, 6:243).

16. For a different perspective of Jefferson's economic view see Joyce Appleby's "Commercial Farming and the 'Agrarian Myth' in the Early Republic" and "The Social Origins of the American Revolutionary Ideology"; in the latter she traces the development of a modern liberal economic theory which existed alongside of the older republican theory. The liberals were in favor of economic growth: "Pushing hard for the acceleration of commercial activities, they became apostles for change—change in the number and kinds of merchants, changes in the tempo and patterns of marketing, change in the range and quantity of goods produced and sold. The acquisitive instinct, long suffered as a barely repressible vice, now shared in the respectibility that naturalness acquired in seventeenth-century thought" (p. 952). Although Bolingbroke, among others, argues "to stay the course of modernization and to forestall an accommodation to the economic development that would undercut the values they esteemed and the social order that supported those values" (p. 952), in my view, Jefferson did not. "Deliverance from the strictures of classical republicanism came from the ideology of liberalism, from a belief in a natural harmony of benignly striving individuals saved from chaos by the stability worked into nature's own design. First expressed in very local clashes over economic rights in the middle decades of the eighteenth-century, this naturalistic recasting of human experience appeared as the universal law of self-interest among radical agitators in the 1760s and

acquired final validation as part of the plan of nature and of nature's God in Thomas Jefferson's apotheosis to individual liberty" (p. 956). That Jefferson had no fear of modernity is true. My disagreement with Appleby is twofold: (1) Jefferson's world view was *non*-capitalist (i.e., neither *anti*- nor *pro*-capitalist); (2) the view of liberalism that she holds seems to be overly optimistic. For a more sober account of liberalism see Sheldon Wolin's *Politics and Vision*, chap. 9, "Liberalism and the Decline of Political Philosophy." It may be useful to view Jefferson as a liberal, but it is more of the organic liberalism of a Rousseau than the atomistic variant, as in Locke.

17. TJ to William H. Crawford, 20 June 1816, *Works of TJ*, 11:538.

18. TJ to James Madison, 8 Dec. 1784, *Papers of TJ*, 7:559.

19. *Notes on Virginia*, p. 164.

20. Ibid., pp. 164-65. Jefferson never seems to appreciate fully the fact that in Virginia it is the slaves who actually "labour in the earth." For a more extensive view of Jefferson and slavery see chapter 4.

21. TJ to George Washington, 14 Aug. 1787, *Papers of TJ*, 12:38.

22. TJ to Plumard DoRieux, 6 Jan. 1792, *Works of TJ*, 6:363.

23. *Notes on Virginia*, p. 165. See also TJ to G. K. Hogendorp, 13 Oct. 1785, *Papers of TJ*, 8:633.

24. *Notes on Virginia*, p. 165.

25. John Locke, *Two Treatises of Government*, ed. Peter Laslett (New York: New American Library, 1963), pp. 338-39. A fuller treatment of Jefferson's views on the fortuitous conditions of the American Indian is continued in the next chapter. Indeed, Jefferson admits that they may be the happiest men in all the world.

26. TJ to Charles Bellini, 30 Sept. 1785, *Papers of TJ*, 8:568. Consider also his letter to Eliza House Twist, 18 Aug. 1785, *Papers of TJ*, 8:404. "Indeed it is difficult to conceive how so good a people, with so good a king, so well disposed rulers in general, so genial a climate, so fertile a soil, should be rendered so ineffectual for producing human happiness by one single curse, that of a bad form of government. But it is a fact. In spite of the mildness of their governors the people are ground to powder by the vices of the form of government. Of twenty millions of people supposed to be in France I am of opinion there are nineteen millions more wretched, more accursed in every circumstance of human existence, than the most conspicuously wretched individual of the whole United States.—I beg your pardon for getting into politics. I will add only one sentiment more of that character. That is, nourish peace with their persons, but war against their manners. Every step we take towards the adoption of their manners is a step towards perfect misery."

27. Ibid., p. 569.

28. Adair, "Intellectual Origins," p. 29, calls it "political agrarianism" to emphasize the positive political consequences of farming.

29. Marx, *Machine in the Garden*, pp. 125-26.

30. Koch, *Jefferson and Madison*, p. 217.

31. *Notes on Virginia*, p. 175.

32. TJ to William Short, 15 Mar. 1787, *Papers of TJ*, 11:215.

33. TJ to John Rutledge, 19 June 1788, *Papers of TJ*, 13:269.

34. TJ to Charles Thomson, 11 Nov. 1784, *Papers of TJ*, 7:519.

35. TJ to Dr. Benjamin Rush, 16 Jan. 1811, *Works of TJ*, 11:168.

36. Wills, *Inventing America*, passim.

37. John Locke, *An Essay Concerning Human Understanding*, ed. A. D. Woozley (London: Wm. Collins Sons & Co. Ltd., 1964), pp. 67, 78, 89.

38. Marx, *Machine in the Garden*, p. 82.

39. Quoted in John Hermann Randall, Jr., *The Making of the Modern Mind*, 50th anniversary ed. (New York: Columbia University Press, 1976), p. 224; see also Marx, *Machine in the Garden*, p. 82.

40. See TJ to Dr. Caspar Wistar, 21 June 1807, *Works of TJ*, 10:423: "I am not a friend to placing growing men in populous cities, because they acquire there habits & partialities which do not contribute to the happiness of their after life."

41. *Notes on Virginia*, pp. 166–68.

42. TJ to Mr. Giroud, 22 May 1797, *The Writings of Thomas Jefferson*, ed. Albert Ellery Bergh, 20 vols. (Washington, D.C.: Thomas Jefferson Memorial Association, 1907), 9:387–88; hereafter cited as *Writings of TJ* (Bergh).

43. TJ to Robert R. Livingston, 16 Feb. 1801, *Works of TJ*, 9:181; see also E. F. Schumacher, *Small Is Beautiful* (New York: Harper & Row, 1973).

44. See the excellent analysis of the tragedy of Jefferson's relationship with the American Indians contained in Bernard W. Sheehan, *Seeds of Extinction: Jeffersonian Philanthropy and the American Indian* (New York: Published for the Institute of Early American History and Culture at Williamsburg, Virginia, by W. W. Norton, 1973).

45. TJ to Handsom Lake, 3 Nov. 1802; TJ to the Miamis and Delawares, 8 Jan. 1803; TJ to Choctaw Nation, 17 Dec. 1803, in *The Complete Jefferson*, ed. Saul K. Padover (Freeport, N.Y.: Books for Libraries Press, 1969), pp. 104–5.

46. TJ to Samuel Kercheval, 12 July 1786, *Works of TJ*, 12:10.

47. TJ to Geismar, 6 Sept. 1785, *Papers of TJ*, 8:500; see also John Chester Miller, *The Wolf by the Ears: Thomas Jefferson and Slavery* (New York: Free Press, 1977), pp. 82–83, where he describes Jefferson's ideal: "If Americans remained an agricultural people, Jefferson assumed they would eschew the pursuit of wealth and power for the modest, down-to-earth but durable pleasures of an American farmer: contentment, independence, and enough land for the needs of his family. This farmer, as Jefferson conceived him, renounced the unending striving for more; he shunned luxuries, never bought on credit, and never went into debt. He recognized that there was no happiness for him on earth unless he restrained his desire for material possessions within the compass of his actual needs, and that he must rest content with a fair share of the earth's

bounty. He combined agriculture with the solid gratifications derived from literature and the contemplation of Nature: 'Ours are the only farmers who read Homer,' boasted Jefferson. The kind of semisubsistence farming practiced by the small yeoman farmers of western Virginia—almost devoid of money, self-sufficient except for a small surplus with which to buy salt, sugar, and coffee 'and a little finery for his [the farmer's] wife and daughters.' In such a society no one would want for the necessities of life and neither would any one get rich.''

48. TJ to Dupont De Nemours, 15 Apr. 1811, *Works of TJ*, 11:199-204; cf. Ronald T. Takaki, *Iron Cages: Race and Culture in Nineteenth-Century America* (New York: Alfred A. Knopf, 1979).

49. TJ to David Humphreys, 23 June 1791, *Works of TJ*, 6:273.

50. ''First Annual Message,'' 8 Dec. 1801, *Works of TJ*, 9:339.

51. TJ to Thomas Leiper, 21 Jan. 1809, *Works of TJ*, 11:91.

52. TJ to Benjamin Austin, 9 Jan. 1816, *Works of TJ*, 11:502-3. In 1817 Jefferson was also revising his position on this. Technology, by using labor-saving devices, was now doing for the artisan what the earth did for the farmer. See TJ to William Sampson, 26 Jan. 1817, *Works of TJ*, 12:49.

53. TJ to Benjamin Austin, 9 Jan. 1816, *Works of TJ*, 11:503.

54. TJ to John Adams, 21 Jan. 1812, *A-J Letters*, p. 291. This tone and style are reminiscent of Rousseau's *First Discourse*.

55. TJ to Benjamin Austin, 9 Jan. 1816, *Works of TJ*, 11:504.

56. TJ to William Short, 28 Nov. 1814, *Writings of TJ* (Bergh), 14:214.

57. TJ to James Madison, 28 Oct. 1785, *Papers of TJ*, 8:681-82. Jefferson, commenting on the high number of unemployed Frenchmen and the considerable portion of uncultivated lands, claims that: ''Whenever there is in any country, uncultivated lands and unemployed poor, it is clear that the laws of property have been so far extended as to violate natural right. The earth is given as a common stock for man to labour and live on. If, for the encouragement of industry we allow it to be appropriated, we must take care that other employment be furnished to those excluded from the appropriation. If we do not the fundamental right to labour the earth returns to the unemployed. It is too soon yet in our country to say that every man who cannot find employment but who can find uncultivated land, shall be at liberty to cultivate it, paying a moderate rent. But it is not too soon to provide by every possible means that as few as possible shall be without a little portion of land.''

58. Jean-Jacques Rousseau, *The Social Contract*, from *The Social Contract*, ed. by Charles M. Sherover, rev. trans. (New York: New American Library, 1974), pp. 271, 85.

59. Macpherson, *Democratic Theory*, p. 135.

60. On many occasions, Jefferson himself uses the Eden metaphor.

61. It is perhaps for these priorities that Jefferson failed to run his own farm profitably. He died nearly in bankruptcy, saved only by the intervention of wealthy friends.

Chapter 4
The Nature of Man: Red, White, and Black

1. TJ to John Adams, 15 June 1813, *A-J Letters*, p. 332.
2. TJ to John Adams, 11 June 1812, *A-J Letters*, pp. 305-6.
3. Jean-Jacques Rousseau, *The First and Second Discourses*, ed. and tr. Roger Master (New York: St. Martin's Press, 1964), p. 103.
4. *Notes on Virginia*, p. 47.
5. Ibid., p. 58.
6. Ibid., pp. 58-59.
7. Ibid., pp. 59-60.
8. See Sheehan *Seeds of Extinction*, pp. 15-44.
9. TJ to Chastellux, 7 June 1785, *Papers of TJ*, 8:185.
10. Ibid.; it must be noted that Jefferson does not rush to make similar claims in defense of slaves.
11. *Notes on Virginia*, p. 62; Sheehan, *Seeds of Extinction*, p. 76.
12. *Notes on Virginia*, pp. 62, 93.
13. TJ to Francis W. Gilmer, 7 June 1816, *Works of TJ*, 11:535.
14. TJ to Peter Carr, 10 Aug. 1787, *Papers of TJ*, 12:14-15.
15. Most scholars on Jefferson interpret the dialogue differently, believing that the Head wins the debate. Their response is symptomatic of the ability of the "traditional" interpretation of Jefferson to color the data to fit the theory (see the introduction). As Julian Boyd presents the case: "This remarkable letter—one of the most revealing in the entire body of TJ's correspondence, and one of the notable love letters in the English language—owes much of its distinction to the fact that its recipient, who unquestionably had captivated TJ momentarily, could not be quite certain whether the Head or the Heart had won the argument, nor avoid the feeling that even the lines given to the Heart to utter were coolly and skilfully contrived by the Head. Her baffled and ineffectual response of 30 Oct. showed an awareness of what the Heart had to say, but little understanding of the essential nature of the man to whom reason was not only enthroned as the chief disciplinarian of his life but also, as revealed in the nature of his response to its commands, was itself a sovereign to whom the Heart yielded a ready and full allegiance, proud of its monarch and happy in his rule" (*Papers of TJ*, 10:453n).
16. TJ to Maria Cosway, 12 Oct. 1786, *Papers of TJ*, 10:444.
17. Ibid., pp. 448-49.
18. Ibid., pp. 449-50.
19. Ibid.
20. Ibid., p. 451.
21. Wills, *Inventing America*, p. 225.
22. TJ to Peter Carr, 10 Aug. 1787, *Papers of TJ*, 12:15.
23. TJ to John Adams, 14 Oct. 1816, *A-J Letters*, p. 492.
24. TJ to Francis W. Gilmer, 7 June 1816, *Writings of TJ* (Bergh), 15:24-25.

See also TJ to Thomas Law, 13 June 1814, *Writings of TJ* (Bergh), 14:142. "The Creator would indeed have been a bungling artist, had He intended man for a social animal, without planting in him social dispositions. It is true they are not planted in every man, because there is no rule without exceptions; but it is false reasoning which converts exceptions into the general rule. Some men are born without the organs of sight, or of hearing, or without hands. Yet it would be wrong to say that man is born without these faculties, and sight, hearing, and hands may with truth enter into the general definition of man. The want or imperfection of the moral sense in some men, like the want or imperfection of the senses of sight and hearing in others, is no proof that it is a general characteristic of the species."

25. TJ to James Fishback, 27 Sept. 1809, *Writings of TJ* (Bergh), 12:315.

26. *Notes on Virginia*, p. 93.

27. In compiling evidence for his report of *Notes on the State of Virginia*, Jefferson contacted many friends and acquaintances. Charles Thomson, veteran observer of Indian life and an adopted member of the Delaware Tribe, was of so much assistance that Jefferson elected to append Thomson's notes to the printed edition of *Notes on the State of Virginia*. Concerning the apparent lack of society among the Indians, Thomson corroborates Jefferson: "But it is said, they are averse to society and a social life. Can any thing be more inapplicable than this to a people who always live in towns or clans? Or can they be said to have no 'republique,' who conduct all their affairs in national councils, who pride themselves in their national character, who consider an insult or injury done to an individual by a stranger as done to the whole, and resent it accordingly? In short, this picture is not applicable to any nation of Indians I have ever known or heard of in North America." And with respect to the position of leadership, Thomson observes: "Their government is a kind of patriarchal confederacy. Every town or family has a chief, who is distinguished by a particular title, and whom we commonly call 'Sachem.' The several towns or families that compose a tribe, have a chief who presides over it, and the several tribes composing a nation have a chief who presides over the whole nation. These chiefs are generally men advanced in years, and distinguished by their prudence and abilities in council. . . . When any matter is proposed in the national council, it is common for the chiefs of the several tribes to consult thereon apart with their counsellors, and, when they have agreed, to deliver the opinion of the tribe at the national council: and, as their government seems to rest wholly on persuasion, they endeavour, by mutual concessions, to obtain unanimity" (*Notes on Virginia*, pp. 202-3). Sheehan, *Seeds of Extinction*, pp. 110-11, quotes the Moravian missionary John Heckewelder to substantiate this point: "The Indian had 'a government in which there are no positive laws, but only long established habits and customs, no code of jurisprudence, but the experience of former times, no magistrates, but advisors, to whom the

people, nevertheless, pay a willing and implicit obedience, in which age confers rank, wisdom gives power, and moral goodness secures a title to universal respect.' ''

28. TJ to James Madison, 30 Jan. 1787, *Papers of TJ*, 11:92–93; see also Sheehan, *Seeds of Extinction*, p. 111.

29. *Notes on Virginia*, p. 93; see TJ to the General Assembly of Virginia, Oct. 1798, *Works of TJ*, 8:451.

30. TJ to Edward Carrington, 16 Jan. 1787, *Papers of TJ*, 11:49.

31. TJ to James Madison, 30 Jan. 1787, *Papers of TJ*, 11:92–93.

32. Ibid.; see also TJ to William Ludlow, 6 Sept. 1824, *Writings of TJ* (Bergh), 16:76: ''A society of seventy families, the number you name, may very possibly be governed as a single family, subsisting on their common industry, and holding all things in common. Some regulators of the family you still must have, and it remains to be seen at what period of your increasing population your simple regulations will cease to be sufficient to preserve order, peace, and justice. The experiment is interesting; I shall not live to see its issue, but I wish it success equal to your hopes.'' See TJ to Cornelius Camden Blatchly, 21 Oct. 1822, *Writings of TJ* (Washington), 7:263: ''That, on the principle of communion of property, small societies may exist in habits of virtue, order, industry, and peace, and consequently in a state of as much happiness as heaven has been pleased to deal out to imperfect humanity, I can readily conceive, and, indeed, have seen its proofs in various small societies which have been constituted on that principle. But I do not feel authorized to conclude from these that an extended society like that of the United States, or of an individual State, could be governed happily on the same principle. I look to the diffusion of light and education as the resource most to be relied on for ameliorating the condition, promoting the virtue, and advancing the happiness of man.''

33. *Notes on Virginia*, p. 93.

34. TJ to Thomas Law, 13 June 1814, *Writings of TJ* (Bergh), 14:140. See Wills, *Inventing America*, p. 292.

35. TJ to James Madison, 28 Aug. 1789, *Works of TJ*, 5:492. It is significant that this rhetorical question is posed to Madison, whose concept of man views individual behavior in direct contrast to man's behavior in a faction, or group.

36. Cf. James Madison, in *Federalist*, no. 51: ''Ambition must be made to counteract ambition. . . . It may be a reflection on human nature that such devices should be necessary. . . . But what is government itself but the greatest of all reflections on human nature? If men were angels, no government would be necessary.'' And yet, Jefferson clearly believes that in some types of societies, ''no government would be necessary.''

37. TJ to William Ludlow, 6 Sept. 1824, *Writings of TJ* (Bergh), 16:74–75. For a different view on Jefferson and the American Indian see Takaki, *Iron Cages*. Takaki's argument begins with the head/heart dichotomy but

mistakenly believes that the head must rule. His treatment reads back into Jefferson the republican paradigm, making Jefferson a spokesman for a "fusion of Protestant asceticism and republican theory," providing "the ideology for bourgeois acquistiveness and modern capitalism" (p. 9). After quoting the same passage from the Jefferson letter to Ludlow, Takaki concludes: "To Jefferson, 'progress' meant the advance from 'savagery' to pastoral and urban civilization, from the past to the present" (p. 57). Takaki pushes too far; his interesting book may be an accurate characterization of the American bourgeois frame of mind, but it is not Jefferson's. The best treatment of Jefferson and the American Indian is found in Sheehan, *Seeds of Extinction*.

38. Arthur O. Lovejoy, *The Great Chain of Being: A Study of the History of an Idea* (Cambridge: Harvard University Press, 1976), pp. 24-66.

39. Malone, *Jefferson and His Time*, 1:440-45.

40. "Declaration of Independence," *Papers of TJ*, 1:317-18.

41. Edmund S. Morgan, *The Challenge of the American Revolution* (New York: W. W. Norton, 1976), p. 167. Morgan estimates that over 50% of the labor force in Virginia in 1700 were slaves.

42. "Declaration of Independence," *Papers of TJ*, 1:353, 363.

43. "A Bill Concerning Slaves," *Papers of TJ*, 2:471; "Jefferson's Draft of A Constitution for Virginia," ibid., 6:298.

44. TJ to Jean Nicolas Démeunier, 26 June 1786, *Papers of TJ*, 10:63. "What a stupendous, what an incomprehensible machine is man! Who can endure toil, famine, stripes, imprisonment or death itself in vindication of his own liberty, and the next moment be deaf to all those motives whose power supported him thro' his trial, and inflict on his fellow men a bondage, one hour of which is fraught with more misery than ages of that which he rose in rebellion to oppose."

45. TJ to Dr. George Logan, 11 May 1805, *Works of TJ*, 10:141.

46. TJ to Edward Coles, 25 Aug. 1814, *Works of TJ*, 11:419.

47. TJ to Nicholas Lewis, 29 July 1787, *Papers of TJ*, 11:640. The best studies of Jefferson and slavery are Jordan Winthrop, *White over Black: American Attitudes toward the Negroe, 1550-1812* (New York: W. W. Norton, 1977), and Miller, *Wolf by the Ears*.

48. TJ to Marquis de Chastellux, 7 June 1785, *Papers of TJ*, 8:185.

49. *Notes on Virginia*, p. 143.

50. Ibid., p. 138.

51. TJ to Marquis de Chastellux, 7 June 1785, *Papers of TJ*, 8:186.

52. "Jefferson's Notes from Condorcet on Slavery," 2 Jan. 1789, *Papers of TJ*, 14:494-98.

53. TJ to the Marquis de Condorcet, 30 Aug. 1791, *Works of TJ*, 6:311; see TJ to Benjamin Banneker, 30 Aug. 1791, ibid., pp. 309-10: "No body wishes more than I do to see such proofs as you exhibit, that nature has given to our black brethren, talents equal to those of the other colors of men, and that the appearance of a want of them is owing merely to the

degraded condition of their existence, both in Africa and America. I can add with truth, that no body wishes more ardently to see a good system commenced for raising the condition both of their body and mind to what it ought to be, as fast as the imbecility of their present existence, and other circumstances which cannot be neglected, will admit"; see also Miller, *Wolf by the Ears*, pp. 76–77.

54. TJ to Henri Grégoire, 25 Feb. 1809, *Works of TJ*, 11:99–100.

55. *Notes on Virginia*, pp. 142–43.

56. TJ to Henri Grégoire, 25 Feb. 1809, *Works of TJ*, 11:100.

57. TJ to William Burwell, 28 Jan. 1805, *Works of TJ*, 10:126.

58. Autobiography (1821), ibid., 1:77; see also TJ to John Adams, 22 Jan. 1821, *A-J Letters*, p. 562.

59. *Notes on Virginia*, p. 163.

60. TJ to Jean Nicolas Démeunier, 26 June 1786, *Papers of TJ*, 10:63.

61. TJ to Chastellux, 7 June 1785, *Papers of TJ*, 8:184.

62. *Notes on Virginia*, p. 163; TJ to David Barrow, 1 May 1815, *Works of TJ*, 11:470–71.

63. *Notes on Virginia*, p. 138; "Autobiography," *Works of TJ*, 1:77; TJ to James Monroe, 20 Sept. 1800, ibid., 9:146; TJ to Jared Sparks, 4 Feb. 1824, ibid., 12:334–39.

64. Slave uprisings in the West Indies alarmed Jefferson. He advises his friends that it is essential that Virginia complete a "peaceable accommodation between justice, policy, & necessity" as soon as possible. The costs of failing such course of action will result in "the murders of our own children" (TJ to St. George Tucker, 28 Aug. 1797, *Works on TJ*, 8:335).

65. TJ to Bishop James Madison, 31 Jan. 1800, *Works of TJ*, 9:108.

66. TJ to John Adams, 15 June 1813, *A-J Letters*, p. 332; this is from the opening quotation to the chapter.

67. TJ to Philip Mazzei, Nov. 1785, *Papers of TJ*, 9:68: "But when commerce began to make progress, when the transfer of property came into daily use, when the modifications of these transfers were infinitely diversified, when with the improvement of other faculties that of the moral sense became also improved, and learnt to respect justice in a variety of cases which it had not formerly discriminated, the instances of injustice left without remedy by courts adhering to the letter of the law, would be so numerous as to produce a general desire that a power should be found somewhere which would redress them."

68. TJ to Samuel Kercheval, 12 July 1816, *Works of TJ*, 12:12.

Chapter 5
Jeffersonian Government: Public and Private Happiness

1. TJ to Samuel Kercheval, 12 July 1816, *Works of TJ*, 12:8–9.

2. TJ to James Madison, 20 Dec. 1787, *Papers of TJ*, 12:438–44; see also TJ to Edward Carrington, 21 Dec. 1787, ibid., pp. 445–47; TJ to Uriah Forrest,

31 Dec. 1787, ibid., pp. 475-79; TJ to William Stephens Smith, 2 Feb. 1788, ibid., pp. 557-59; TJ to Alexander Donald, 7 Feb. 1788, ibid., pp. 570-72; TJ to James Madison, 31 July 1788, ibid., 13:440-43; TJ to James Madison, 15 Mar. 1789, ibid., 14:659-63; and in a letter to Dr. Joseph Priestley, 19 June 1802, *Works of TJ*, 9:381, Jefferson goes out of his way to see that history records the fact that he had no part to play in either the drafting or the passing of the Constitution of 1787.

3. *Papers of TJ*, 1:330.

4. TJ to Samuel Kercheval, 12 July 1816, *Works of TJ*, 12:4-7; see also TJ to John Taylor, 28 May 1816, *Works of TJ*, 11:532-33.

5. *Notes on Virginia*, p. 118.

6. TJ to John Taylor, 28 May 1816, *Works of TJ*, 11:531; see also TJ to John Hambden Pleasants, 19 Apr. 1824, ibid., 12:353.

7. *Notes on Virginia*, p. 118; cf. John Stuart Mill's *"Considerations on Representative Government in Utilitarianism," "On Liberty," and "Considerations on Representative Government"* (London: J. M. Dent & Sons Ltd., 1972), chap. 8. Here Mill argues for a plural voting scheme along with the exclusion of others from any vote at all.

8. "Jefferson's Third Draft," *Papers of TJ*, 1:348, 362; TJ has filled in the amounts in parentheses at a later time.

9. "Revision of Virginia Constitution 1782," *Papers of TJ*, 6:296.

10. TJ to Samuel Kercheval, 12 July 1816, *Works of TJ*, 12:9; see also "Notes for a Constitution," 1794, ibid., 8:159; TJ to Jeremiah Mor, 14 Aug. 1800, ibid., 9:142; and TJ to Edmund Pendleton, 26 Aug. 1776, *Papers of TJ*, 1:504.

11. TJ to Samuel Kercheval, 5 Sept. 1816, *Works of TJ*, 12:15; TJ to John Hambden Pleasants, 19 Apr. 1824, ibid., 12:353.

12. TJ to Governor Tyler, 26 May 1810, *Writings of TJ*, 5:525-26.

13. TJ to Joseph C. Cabell, 2 Feb. 1816, *Writings of TJ*, 6:543. See TJ to Samuel Kercheval, 12 July 1816, *Works of TJ*, 12:9, where he describes the pattern in these terms: "We should thus marshal our government into, 1. the general federal republic, for all concerns foreign and federal; 2. that of the State, for what relates to our own citizens exclusively; 3. the county republics, for the duties and concerns of the county; and 4. the ward republics, for the small, and yet numerous and interesting concerns of the neighborhood; and in government, as well as in every other business of life, it is by division and subdivision of duties alone, that all matters, great and small, can be managed to perfection. And the whole is cemented by giving to every citizen, personally, a part in the administration of the public affairs."

14. TJ to Samuel Kercheval, 12 July 1816, *Works of TJ*, 12:9.

15. TJ to Joseph C. Cabell, 2 Feb. 1816, *Writings of TJ*, 6:543-44.

16. Ibid., p. 543.

17. TJ to Samuel Kercheval, 12 July 1816, *Works of TJ*, 12:5; and, TJ to Samuel Kercheval, 5 Sept. 1816, ibid., 12:15.

18. TJ to Samuel Kercheval, 12 July 1816, *Works of TJ*, 12:8. Jefferson's fascination with the ward-republics was undoubtedly influenced by his own observation and knowledge of the American Indian. In his *Notes on Virginia* Jefferson published some editorial comments by the secretary of Congress, Charles Thomson. Note the similarity in Thomson's account of tribal "government" and Jefferson's writings on ward-republics. "The matters which merely regard a town or family are settled by the chief and principal men of the town: those which regard a tribe, such as the appointment of head warriors or captains, and settling differences between different towns and families, are regulated at a meeting or council of the chiefs from the several towns; and those which regard the whole nation, such as the making war, concluding peace, or forming alliances with the neighbouring nations, are deliberated on and determined in a national council composed of the chiefs of the tribe, attended by the head warriors and a number of the chiefs from the towns, who are his counsellors. In every town there is a council house, where the chief and old men of the town assemble, when occasion requires, and consult what is proper to be done. Every tribe has a fixed place for the chiefs of the towns to meet and consult on the business of the tribe: and in every nation there is what they call the central council house, or central council fire, where the chiefs of the several tribes, with the principal warriors, convene to consult and determine on their national affairs" (p. 203).

19. Adrienne Koch, *The Philosophy of Thomas Jefferson* (Chicago: Quadrangle Books, 1964), pp. 162–65.

20. Arendt, *On Revolution*, pp. 238, 235; see also Rousseau's *Social Contract*, p. 161: "The English people think that it is free, but is greatly mistaken, for it is so only during the election of members of Parliament; as soon as they are elected, it is enslaved and counts for nothing."

21. TJ to Samuel Kercheval, 12 July 1816, *Works of TJ*, 12:11; see also chap. 2 above.

22. TJ to Samuel Kercheval, 12 July 1816, *Works of TJ*, 12:14.

23. Ibid., and TJ to Samuel Kercheval, 15 Sept. 1816, ibid., 12:15; cf. *Notes on Virginia*, p. 149.

24. TJ to James Madison, 30 Jan. 1787, *Papers of TJ*, 11:93.

25. TJ to William Stephens Smith, 13 Nov. 1787, *Papers of TJ*, 12:356–57; see also TJ to Abigail Adams, 22 Feb. 1787, ibid., 11:174.

26. TJ to John Adams, 4 Sept. 1823, *A-J Letters*, pp. 596–97; see also TJ to John Adams, 12 Sept. 1821, ibid., pp. 574–76.

27. Arendt, *On Revolution*, pp. 252–53; see chap. 1 above.

28. TJ to Joseph C. Cabell, 2 Feb. 1816, *Writings of TJ*, 6:544.

29. TJ to Judge Spencer Roane, 6 Sept. 1819, *Works of TJ*, 12:137.

30. TJ to John Adams, 25 Nov. 1816, *A-J Letters*, p. 497.

31. TJ to William Findley, 24 Mar. 1801, *Works of TJ*, 9:225.

32. "Jefferson's Opinion on the Constitutionality of the Residence Bill, 1790," *Papers of TJ*, 17:195.

33. TJ to Richard Price, 8 Jan. 1789, ibid., 14:420.

34. TJ to William Charles Jarvis, 28 Sept. 1820, *Works of TJ*, 12:163.

35. TJ to George Wythe, 13 Aug. 1786, *Papers of TJ*, 10:244.

36. See "Jefferson's Epitaph," *Works of TJ*, 12:483; TJ to George Ticknor, 25 Nov. 1817, ibid., 12:77–79; TJ to Joseph C. Cabell, 28 Nov. 1820, ibid., 12:171; "Jefferson's Autobiography," ibid., 1:75–76; *Notes on Virginia*, p. 146.

37. Arendt, *On Revolution*, p. 129; see Hannah Arendt, *The Human Condition* (Chicago: University of Chicago Press, 1974), pp. 22–78.

38. TJ to James Madison, 9 June 1793, *Writings of TJ* (Bergh), 9:119.

39. J. G. A. Pocock, *Politics, Language and Time: Essays on Political Thought and History* (New York: Atheneum, 1971), p. 85.

40. Kramnick, "Republican Revisionism," p. 630.

41. Pocock, *Machiavellian Moment*, p. 56. Hannah Arendt, in *The Human Condition*, claims that the *vita activa*, to the Greeks, was specifically a public concern.

42. TJ to David Rittenhouse, 19 July 1778, *Works of TJ*, 2:345. Perhaps it is someone like Franklin or Rittenhouse whom Aristotle is refering to when he writes: "He who is without a polis, by reason of his own nature and not of some accident, is either a poor sort of being, or a being higher than man" (Book 1 of *The Politics*).

43. TJ to James Monroe, 20 May 1782, *Works of TJ*, 3:300–301.

44. TJ to William Short, 31 Oct. 1819, ibid., 12:142.

45. TJ to Benjamin Rush, 21 Apr. 1803, ibid., 9:457; see also TJ to John Adams, 11 Apr. 1823, *A-J Letters*, p. 591.

46. TJ to William Short, 31 Oct. 1819, *Works of TJ*, 12:145.

47. J. M. Rist, *Epicurus: An Introduction* (Cambridge: Cambridge University Press, 1972), p. 102.

48. TJ to William Short, 31 Oct. 1819, *Works of TJ*, 12:145.

49. Rist, *Epicurus*, pp. 130, 133.

50. TJ to John Adams, 7 Nov. 1819, *A-J Letters*, pp. 546–47.

51. TJ to Charles Thompson, 9 Jan. 1816, *Works of TJ*, 11:498; see also TJ to Benjamin Rush, 21 Apr. 1803, ibid., 9:457.

52. TJ to William Short, 31 Oct. 1819, ibid., 12:142.

53. TJ to John Adams, 11 Apr. 1823, *A-J Letters*, p. 594.

54. TJ to Dr. Benjamin Waterhouse, 26 June 1822, *Works of TJ*, 12:241–42.

55. TJ to George Thacker, 26 Jan. 1824, ibid., 12:332.

56. TJ to Benjamin Rush, 21 Apr. 1803, ibid., 9:462–63.

57. TJ to John Adams, 11 Apr. 1823, *A-J Letters*, p. 592.

58. Koch, *Philosophy of Thomas Jefferson*, p. 42.

Chapter 6
Jefferson in the American Context: The Liberalism of Madison and Hamilton

1. TJ to James Madison, 28 Aug. 1789, *Works of TJ*, 5:92; *Federalist*, no. 55, p. 374; *Federalist*, no. 15, p. 96.

2. The contribution of John Jay is so marginal that he does not enter as a factor.

3. See Garry Wills, *Explaining America*. He, too, observes the similarities; part 1 of his book is called "The 'Hamiltonian' Madison," and part 2 is called "The 'Madisonian' Hamilton" to emphasize this point.

4. Marvin Meyers, ed., *The Mind of the Founder: Sources of the Political Thought of James Madison* (Indianapolis and New York: Bobbs-Merrill Co., Inc., 1973), p. 215.

5. Meyers, *Mind*, p. 512. Hamilton holds a similar perspective. Prior to civil society, he argues, "no man had any *moral* power to deprive another of his life, limbs, property, or liberty" (*The Works of Alexander Hamilton*, ed. Henry Cabot Lodge, 12 vols. [New York: G. P. Putnam's Sons, 1903], 1:63; hereafter cited as *Works of AH*). Moreover, everybody has a natural right to protect himself. "Self-preservation is the first principle of our nature. When our lives and our properties are at stake, it would be foolish and unnatural to refrain from such measures as might preserve them because they would be detrimental to others" (*Works of AH*, 1:12). Even though self-preservation is the "first principle," the desire to protect private property is an equally motivating factor. Indeed, so intimate is the connection between property and society in Hamilton's mind that he states: "The notion of property seems always to imply a contract between the society and the individual, that he shall retain and be protected in the possession and use of his property so long as he shall observe and perform the conditions which the laws have annexed to the tenure" (*Works of AH*, 5:415). For all of these reasons, men make a social contract, "a voluntary compact between the rulers and the ruled" (*Works of AH*, 1:63).

6. Meyers, *Mind*, p. 243; see Blackstone, *Commentaries*, bk. 2, p. 2.

7. Ibid., p. 244.

8. Ibid., p. 245.

9. It should be briefly noted that Madison has two interesting passages in "Property" that could be, if construed broadly, used to show that he did indeed see some sort of tension. "That is not a just government," writes Madison, "nor is property secure under it, where the property which a man has in his personal safety and personal liberty is violated by the arbitrary seizures of one class of citizens for the service of the rest" (Meyers, *Mind*, p. 244). Madison also states: "That is not a just government, nor is property secure under it, where arbitrary restrictions, exemptions, and monopolies deny to part of its citizens that free use of their faculties and free choice of their occupations which not only constitute their property in the general sense of the word, but are the means of acquiring property strickly so called" (p. 245). In view of these quotes, one wonders what Madison would say to an empirical analysis that would demonstrate (1) that an army of wage-laborers is, in a sense, "seized" for "the service of the rest"; and (2) that a "monopoly" of the means of production does indeed deny a majority of men the "free use of

their faculties," which is necessary to their "acquiring property strickly so called."

10. See Martin Diamond's "The Federalist," in *The History of Political Philosophy*, ed. Leo Strauss and Joseph Cropsey (Chicago: Rand McNally, 1974), pp. 631–51; and his "Democracy and the Federalist: A Reconsideration of the Framers' Intent," *American Political Science Review* 53 (1959): 52–68. For a contrasting view that delineates some of the differences between Madison and Hamilton see Forrest McDonald, *Alexander Hamilton: A Biography* (New York: W. W. Norton & Co., 1979), pp. 108–13.

11. *Federalist*, no. 10, p. 57; cf. Hamilton's no. 6.

12. Ibid., no. 14, p. 83.

13. Ibid., no. 10, p. 58.

14. Ibid.

15. Ibid.

16. Ibid.

17. Ibid., p. 59.

18. Ibid.

19. Ibid., pp. 58–59. In a speech during the Constitutional Convention, Hamilton also captures this notion. "Take mankind in general, they are vicious. . . . Our prevailing passions are ambition and interest; and it will ever be the duty of a wise government to avail itself of those passions, in order to make them subservient to the public good" (*The Records of the Federal Convention of 1787*, ed. Max Farrand, rev. ed., 3 vols. [New Haven, Conn.: Yale University Press, 1966], 1:381; hereafter cited as Farrand, *Records*). To say that all men are vicious and self-interested, however, is not to say that they are equally so. Though all ranks in society have their particular vices, the vices of the rich are less dangerous to the nation. The qualitative difference in the type of depravity found in the rich, as contrasted with the poor, is no small matter of political import. In a speech at the convention, Hamilton asserts: "Experience has by no means justified us in the supposition that there is more virtue in one class of men than another. Look through the rich and the poor of the community; the learned and the ignorant. Where does virtue predominate? The difference indeed consists, not in the quantity, but kind of vices, which are incident to the various classes; and here the advantage of character belongs to the wealthy. Their vices are probably more favorable to the prosperity of the state than those of the indigent and partake less of moral depravity" (Farrand, *Records*, 1:436). Hence, the rich should be the governing class, and the foundation for a stable state. In yet another constitutional oration, Hamilton unabashedly puts it this way: "All communities divide themselves into the few and the many. The first are the rich and the well born, the other the mass of the people. The voice of the people has been said to be the voice of God; and however generally this maxim has been quoted and believed, it is not true in fact. The people are turbulent and changing; they seldom judge or determine right. Give therefore to the first class a

distinct, permanent share in the government" (Farrand, *Records*, 1:299).

20. *Federalist*, no. 51, p. 349; Arthur O. Lovejoy, *Reflections on Human Nature* (Baltimore, Md.: Johns Hopkins Press, 1961), p. 41. Lovejoy compares this method to Mandeville's *The Fable of the Bees:* "Though every part was full of Vice / Yet the whole Mass a Paradise / Such were the Blessings of that State / Then crimes conspire to make them great."

21. *Works of AH*, 1:16.

22. Ibid., p. 119.

23. Ibid., p. 285; *Federalist*, no. 6, p. 54.

24. Trevor Colburn, ed., *Fame and the Founding Fathers: Essays by Douglass Adair* (New York: W. W. Norton & Co., 1974), p. 103 and passim.

25. *Federalist*, no. 10, p. 65.

26. Adair, *Fame*, p. 98.

27. Ibid., pp. 99–100.

28. *Federalist*, no. 10, p. 64.

29. Ibid., no. 51, p. 351.

30. Meyers, *Mind*, p. 49.

31. Farrand, *Records*, 2:203.

32. Ibid., 1:432, 143–44.

33. Thomas R. Dye and L. Harmon Zeigler, *The Irony of Democracy: An Uncommon Introduction to American Politics*, 2d ed. (Belmont, Calif.: Wadsworth Publishing Co., Inc., 1972), pp. 42–43.

34. Article 1, section 2, paragraph 1, of the United States Constitution.

35. *Federalist*, no. 57, p. 385.

36. Ibid., no. 52, pp. 354–55.

37. Ibid., no. 54, p. 369.

38. Dye and Zeigler, *Irony*, p. 44.

39. Meyers, *Mind*, p. 502.

40. Ibid., p. 503.

41. Ibid., p. 506.

42. Ibid., p. 507.

43. Ibid., pp. 508–9.

44. *Federalist*, no. 49, p. 340.

45. Ibid.

46. Ibid., no. 55, p. 374; cf. the opening quote by TJ.

47. Meyers, *Mind*, pp. 241–42.

48. Ibid., pp. 242–43.

49. Ibid., p. 243.

50. McCoy, *Elusive Republic*, p. 259.

51. Meyers, *Mind*, p. 504.

52. Ibid.

53. *Federalist*, no. 41, pp. 276–77.

54. Meyers, *Mind*, p. 453, 454.

55. Ibid., p. 517.

56. Ibid., p. 454.

57. A vigorous centralized government with unlimited powers is the Hamiltonian prescription for the human condition. Sound government must be based on a realistic concept of man "because the passions of men will not conform to the dictates of reason and justice, without constraint": anything less than this bulwark would be sheer folly, against the dictates of both reason and history (*Federalist*, no. 15, p. 96).

At the Constitutional Convention, Hamilton explicitly argues that both the executive and the upper house of the legislature must "hold their places for life"; he also argues that the central government must possess the "unlimited power of passing all laws without exception," while the chief executive should "have the power of negating all laws" (*Works of AH*, 1:289, 300). Rebuffed in his oral efforts to bring some sense of permanency to the Constitution, Hamilton left Philadelphia in disgust. Before leaving, however, he submitted to the convention a detailed plan of government.

In his outline there are three separate—but by no means equal—branches of government. With a bicameral legislature, the lower house—called the Assembly—is to sit for three-year terms and is to be elected by "the free male citizens and inhabitants of the several States . . . all of whom of the age of twenty one years and upwards." The election process in the Senate is far more complicated: the citizens of each state are to select "electors," who in turn would elect the senators. But the "electors" have to own a substantial amount of property to qualify for their positions. Not surprisingly, the election of the powerful Hamiltonian president is even more restricted than that of the Senate. It is three times removed from the people (Farrand, *Records*, 3:620–23).

In his draft, both the senators and the president are to have life terms. The legislature, furthermore, may pass all laws, excepting the following: bills of attainder, ex post facto laws, titles of nobility, and religious qualifications for office (Farrand, *Records*, 3:627–28). These exceptions compose what can be called Hamilton's bill of rights. In all candor, they are almost as broad as those finally adopted by Madison et al. in the Constitution per se. The chief difference between Hamilton and Madison on the matters concerning the scope of government is not the protection of individual rights but the degree and kind of state power. While Hamilton believes that government must have carte blanche if it is to rule effectively, Madison holds that it must be limited to certain expressed powers only. It is essential to note that it is Jefferson alone, conveniently tucked away as minister to France, who vehemently protests the lack of a bill of rights in the constitution that was adopted.

In regard to federalism, according to Hamilton's model, the states are to become but administrative arms of the central government; he does not want power to be diversified. "We must," he states, "establish a general and national government, completely sovereign, and annihilate the state distinctions and state operations" (Farrand, *Records*, 1:296). In Hamilton's plan, the president of each state can negate all laws passed within the confines of his state; and even if a particular bill becomes law in a state, the chief executive of the central government can, at his pleasure, negate it (Farrand, *Records*, 3:628).

This is the Hamiltonian scheme of government. It is his advocacy of the necessity of absolute power on the part of the sovereign, rather than any explicit advocacy of a self-perpetuating monarch, that makes him a disciple of Hobbes. Indeed, Hamilton considered himself a republican, not a monarchist. "It may be asked is this [his plan] a republican system? It is strictly so, as long as they remain elective. . . . It may be said this constitutes an elective monarchy? Pray what is a monarch . . . by making the Executive subject to impeachment, the term monarchy cannot apply" (Farrand, *Records*, 1:300).

58. Weber, *Protestant Ethic*.

59. Also noting Hamilton's propensity to deal "with the 'how' " rather than the "why" of government, Clinton Rossiter believes that it is more appropriate to call Hamilton a political theorist rather than a political philosopher. See Jacob Cooke, ed., *Alexander Hamilton: A Profile* (New York: Hill & Wang, 1967), p. 187.

60. Jacob Cooke, ed., *The Reports of Alexander Hamilton* (New York: Harper & Row, 1964), p. 6 (hereafter cited as Cooke, *Reports*).

61. Ibid., p. 48; see also McDonald, *Alexander Hamilton*, pp. 117–236.

62. *Federalist*, no. 30, p. 188.

63. Cooke, *Reports*, p. 48.

64. Vernon L. Parrington, "Hamilton and the Leviathan State," in Cooke, *Alexander Hamilton: A Profile*, p. 145.

65. Cooke, *Reports*, p. 69.

66. Ibid., p. 118.

67. Ibid., p. 121.

68. Ibid., p. 130.

69. Ibid., p. 131.

70. Ibid.

71. Ibid., p. 129.

72. Ibid., p. 164.

73. Cooke, *Alexander Hamilton: A Profile*, p. 71.

74. Cooke, *Reports*, p. 141.

75. *Federalist*, no. 11, p. 68; and Cooke, *Reports*, p. 87.

76. *Federalist*, no. 11, p. 73.

77. Cooke, *Reports*, p. 88.

78. Wood, *Creation*, p. 562.

Chapter 7
Jefferson's Political Philosophy Revisited:
Life, Liberty, and the Pursuit of Happiness

1. TJ to John Adams, 1 Aug. 1816, *A-J Letters*, p. 485.
2. Pocock, *Machiavellian Moment*, p. 533.
3. TJ to P. S. Dupont de Nemours, 24 Apr. 1816, *Works of TJ*, 11:522.
4. Pocock, *Machiavellian Moment*, p. 545.
5. Macpherson, *Political Theory*, p. 270.
6. Ibid., p. 256.
7. Macpherson, *Democratic Theory*, pp. 120–40.
8. Pocock, *Politics, Language, and Time*, p. 103, and *Machiavellian Moment*, p. 551.
9. Rousseau, *First and Second Discourses*, pp. 151–52.
10. Marx, *Machine in the Garden*, pp. 139–40.
11. Macpherson, *Democratic Theory*, p. 5.

Selected Bibliography

Adair, Douglass Greybill. *Fame and the Founding Fathers: Essays by Douglass Adair.* Edited by H. Trevor Colbourn. New York: Published for the Institute of Early American History and Culture, Williamsburg, Virginia, by W. W. Norton & Co., 1974.

———. "The Intellectual Origins of Jeffersonian Democracy: Republicanism, the Class Struggle, and the Virtuous Farmer." Ph.D. diss., Yale University, 1943; also, Ann Arbor, Mich.: University Microfilms International.

Adams, Henry. *Henry Adams: The Education of Henry Adams, and Other Selected Writings.* Abridged and edited by Edward N. Saveth. New York: Washington Square Press, Inc., 1963.

Appleby, Joyce Oldham. "America as a Model for the Radical French Reformers of 1789." *William and Mary Quarterly* 28 (Apr. 1971): 267–86.

———. *Capitalism and a New Social Order: The Republican Vision of the 1790s.* New York and London: New York University Press, 1983.

———. "Commercial Farming and the 'Agrarian Myth' in the Early Republic." *Journal of American History* 68 (Mar. 1982): 833–49.

———. *Economic Thought and Ideology in Seventeenth-Century England.* Princeton, N.J.: Princeton University Press, 1978.

———. "The Social Origins of American Revolutionary Ideology." *Journal of American History* 64 (Mar. 1978): 935–58.

———. "What Is Still American in the Political Philosophy of Thomas Jefferson?" *William and Mary Quarterly* 39 (Apr. 1982): 287–309.

Arendt, Hannah. *The Human Condition.* Chicago: University of Chicago Press, 1974.

———. *On Revolution.* New York: Viking Press, 1963.

Bailyn, Bernard. "The Central Themes of the American Revolution: An Interpretation." In *Essays on the American Revolution,* edited by Stephen G. Kurtz and James H. Hutson, pp. 3–31. Chapel Hill and New York: Published for the Institute of Early American History and Culture,

Williamsburg, Virginia, by the University of North Carolina Press and
W. W. Norton & Co., Inc., 1973.
————. *The Ideological Origins of the American Revolution.* Cambridge:
Belknap Press of Harvard University Press, 1967.
————. *The Origins of American Politics.* New York: Alfred A. Knopf, 1970.
————, ed., *Pamphlets of the American Revolution, 1750–1776.* Cambridge:
Belknap Press of Harvard University Press, 1965–.
Banning, Lance. *The Jeffersonian Persuasion: Evolution of a Party Ideology.*
Ithaca, N.Y.: Published for the Institute of Early American History and
Culture, Williamsburg, Virginia, by Cornell University Press, 1978.
Beard, Charles A. *American Government and Politics.* 8th ed. New York:
Macmillan Co., 1939.
————. *An Economic Interpretation of the Constitution of the United States.*
New York: Macmillan Co., 1913 and 1935.
————. *Economic Origins of Jeffersonian Democracy.* New York: Macmillan
Co., 1915.
————. *The Republic: Conversations on Fundamentals.* New York: Viking
Press, 1943.
Becker, Carl L. *The Declaration of Independence: A Study in the History of
Political Ideas.* New York: Random House, 1958.
Beitzinger, Alfons J. *A History of American Political Thought.* New York:
Dodd, Mead & Co., 1972.
Bell, Daniel. *The End of Ideology: On the Exhaustion of Political Ideas in the
Fifties.* Glencoe, Ill.: Free Press, 1960.
Beloff, Max. *Thomas Jefferson and American Democracy.* London: Hodder &
Stoughton Ltd., 1948.
Blackstone, William. *Commentaries on the Laws of England.* Vol. 2. Oxford:
Clarendon Press, 1765.
Boorstin, Daniel. *The Americans: The Colonial Experience.* New York: Ran-
dom House, 1958.
————. *The Genius of American Politics.* Chicago: University of Chicago
Press, 1953.
————. *The Lost World of Thomas Jefferson.* New York: Henry Holt & Co.,
1948.
Boyd, Julian P., ed. *The Declaration of Independence: The Evolution of the Text.*
. . . Princeton, N.J.: Princeton University Press, 1945.
Buel, Richard, Jr. *Securing the Revolution: Ideology in American Politics,
1789–1815.* Ithaca, N.Y.: Cornell University Press, 1972.
Cappon, Lester J., ed. *The Adams-Jefferson Letters.* New York: Simon &
Schuster, 1971.
Carpenter, William Seal. *The Development of American Political Thought.*
Princeton, N.J.: Princeton University Press, 1930.
Chaudhuri, Joyotpaul, ed. *The Non-Lockean Roots of American Democratic
Thought.* Tucson: University of Arizona Press, 1977.
————. ''Possession, Ownership and Access: A Jeffersonian View of
Property.'' *Political Inquiry* 1, no. 1 (Fall 1973): 78–95.

Chinard, Gilbert. *Thomas Jefferson: The Apostle of Americanism.* Boston: Little, Brown & Co., 1929.

———, ed. *The Commonplace Book of Thomas Jefferson: A Repertory of His Ideas on Government.* Baltimore, Md.: Johns Hopkins Press, 1926.

———, ed. *The Correspondence of Jefferson and Dupont de Nemours.* Baltimore, Md.: Johns Hopkins Press, 1931.

———, ed. *The Letters of Lafayette and Jefferson.* Baltimore, Md.: Johns Hopkins Press, 1929.

Coleman, Frank M. "The Hobbesian Basis of American Constitutionalism." *Polity* 7, no. 1 (Fall 1974): 57–89.

Conlin, Paul K. *Self-Evident Truths: Being a Discourse on the Origins & Development of the First Principles of American Government. . . .* Bloomington: Indiana University Press, 1974.

Cooke, Jacob E. *Alexander Hamilton.* New York: Charles Scribner's Sons, 1982.

———. *Alexander Hamilton: A Profile.* New York: Hill & Wang, 1967.

Dahl, Robert A. *A Preface to Democratic Theory.* Chicago: University of Chicago Press, 1964.

Diamond, Martin. "Democracy and *The Federalist*: A Reconsideration of the Framers' Intent." *American Political Science Review* 53, no. 1 (Mar. 1959): 52–68.

———. "The Federalist." In *History of Political Philosophy,* edited by Leo Strauss and Joseph Cropsey, pp. 631–51. 2d ed. Chicago: Rand McNally, 1972.

Dye, Thomas R., and Zeigler, L. Harmon. *The Irony of Democracy: An Uncommon Introduction to American Politics.* 2d ed. Belmont, Calif.: Wadsworth Publishing Co., Inc., 1972.

Eidelberg, Paul. *On the Silence of the Declaration of Independence.* Amherst: University of Massachusetts Press, 1976.

Ellis, Richard E. *The Jeffersonian Crisis: Courts and Politics in the Young Republic.* New York: Oxford University Press, 1971.

Farrand, Max, ed. *The Records of the Federal Convention of 1787.* Rev. ed. 3 vols. New Haven, Conn.: Yale University Press, 1966.

Ferguson, Adam. *An Essay on the History of Civil Society, 1767.* Edited by Duncan Forbes. Edinburgh: Edinburgh University Press, 1966.

Griswold, A. Whitney. "The Agrarian Democracy of Thomas Jefferson." *American Political Science Review* 40, no. 4 (Aug. 1946): 657–81.

Hamilton, Alexander; Jay, John; and Madison, James. *The Federalist.* Edited by Jacob E. Cooke. 1st paperback ed. Middletown, Conn.: Wesleyan University Press, 1982.

Hamilton, Alexander. *The Reports of Alexander Hamilton.* Edited by Jacob E. Cooke. New York: Harper & Row, 1964.

———. *The Works of Alexander Hamilton.* Edited by Henry Cabot Lodge. 12 vols. New York: C. P. Putnam's Sons, 1903.

Hamowy, Ronald. "Jefferson and the Scottish Enlightenment: A Critique

of Garry Wills's *Inventing America: Jefferson's Declaration of Independence."
William and Mary Quarterly* 36, no. 4 (Oct. 1979): 503–23.

Hartz, Louis. *The Founding of New Societies: Studies in the History of the United States, Latin America, South Africa, Canada and Australia.* New York: Harcourt, Brace, & World, Inc., 1964.

———. *The Liberal Tradition in America: An Interpretation of American Political Thought since the Revolution.* New York: Harcourt, Brace & Co., 1955.

———. "The Rise of the Democratic Idea." In *Paths of American Thought,* edited by Arthur M. Schlesinger, Jr., and Morton White, pp. 37–51. London: Chatto & Windus, 1964.

Higham, John. "Beyond Consensus: The Historian as Moral Critic." *American Historical Review* 67, no. 3 (Apr. 1962): 609–25.

———. "The Cult of the 'American Consensus': Homogenizing Our History." *Commentary* 27 (Feb. 1959): 93–100.

Hofstadter, Richard. *The Age of Reform: From Bryan to F.D.R.* New York: Alfred A. Knopf, 1955.

———. *America at 1750: A Social Portrait.* New York: Random House, 1973.

———. *The American Political Tradition and the Men Who Made It.* New York: Random House, 1973.

———. *The Progressive Historians: Turner, Beard, Parrington.* New York: Alfred A. Knopf, 1968.

Honeywell, Roy J. *The Educational Work of Thomas Jefferson.* New York: Russell & Russell, Inc., 1964.

Howe, Daniel Walker. "European Sources of Political Ideas in Jeffersonian America." *Reviews in American History,* Dec. 1982, pp. 28–44.

Ignatieff, Michael. *A Just Measure of Pain: The Penitentiary in the Industrial Revolution, 1750–1850.* New York: Pantheon Books, 1978.

Ingersoll, David E. "Machiavelli and Madison: Perspectives on Political Stability." *Political Science Quarterly* 85, no. 2 (June 1970): 259–80.

Jaffa, Harry V. "Conflicts within the Idea of the Liberal Tradition." *Comparative Studies in Society and History* 5, no. 3 (Apr. 1963): 274–78.

Jefferson, Thomas. *The Complete Anas of Thomas Jefferson.* Edited by Franklin B. Sawvel. New York: Round Table Press, 1903.

———. *The Complete Jefferson.* Edited by Saul K. Padover. Freeport, N.Y.: Books for Libraries Press, 1969.

———. *Jefferson Himself: The Personal Narrative of a Many-sided American.* Edited by Bernard Mayo. Boston: Houghton Mifflin Co., 1942.

———. *The Life and Morals of Jesus of Nazareth.* New York: Wilfred Funk, Inc., 1940.

———. *Notes on the State of Virginia.* Edited by William Peden. New York: W. W. Norton, 1972.

———. *The Papers of Thomas Jefferson.* Edited by Julian P. Boyd. 20 vols. Princeton, N.J.: Princeton University Press, 1950–82.

———. *The Works of Thomas Jefferson.* Edited by Paul Leicester Ford. 12 vols. New York: Knickerbocker Press, 1904.

————. *The Writings of Thomas Jefferson*. Edited by Albert Ellery Bergh. 20 vols. Washington, D.C.: Thomas Jefferson Memorial Association, 1903–4.

————. *The Writings of Thomas Jefferson*. Edited by H. A. Washington. 9 vols. Washington, D.C.: Washington, Taylor & Maury, 1853–54.

Jordan, Winthrop D. *White over Black: American Attitudes toward the Negro, 1550–1812*. New York: W. W. Norton, 1977.

Kaplan, Lawrence S. *Jefferson and France: An Essay on Politics and Political Ideas*. New Haven, Conn.: Yale University Press, 1967.

Kenyon, Cecelia M. "Alexander Hamilton: Rousseau of the Right." *Political Science Quarterly* 73, no. 2 (June 1958): 161–78.

Ketcham, Ralph L. "James Madison and the Nature of Man." *Journal of the History of Ideas* 19, no. 1 (Jan. 1958): 62–76.

————. "Notes on James Madison's Sources for the Tenth Federalist Paper." *Midwest Journal of Political Science* 1, no. 1 (May 1957): 20–25.

Koch, Adrienne. *Jefferson and Madison: The Great Collaboration*. New York: Oxford University Press, 1976.

————. *Madison's "Advice to My Country."* Princeton, N.J.: Princeton University Press, 1966.

————. *The Philosophy of Thomas Jefferson*. Chicago: Quadrangle Books, 1964.

Kramnick, Isaac. *Bolingbroke and His Circle: The Politics of Nostalgia in the Age of Walpole*. Cambridge: Harvard University Press, 1968.

————. "Republican Revisionism Revisited." *American Historical Review* 87, no. 3 (June 1982): 629–64.

Kuhn, Thomas S. *The Structure of Scientific Revolutions*. 2d ed., enl. London and Chicago: University of Chicago Press, 1970.

Kurtz, Stephen G., and Hutson, James H., eds. *Essays on the American Revolution*. Chapel Hill: Published for the Institute of Early American History and Culture, Williamsburg, Virginia, by the University of North Carolina Press, 1973.

Lea, James F. *Political Consciousness and American Democracy*. Jackson: University Press of Mississippi, 1982.

Levy, Leonard W. *Jefferson & Civil Liberties: The Darker Side*. Cambridge: Belknap Press of Harvard University Press, 1963.

Locke, John. *An Essay Concerning Human Understanding*. Edited by A. D. Woozley. London: William Collins Sons & Co. Ltd., 1964.

————. *Two Treatises of Government*. Edited by Peter Laslett. New York: New American Library, 1963.

Lovejoy, Arthur O. *The Great Chain of Being: A Study of the History of an Idea*. Cambridge, Harvard University Press, 1976.

————. *Reflections on Human Nature*. Baltimore, Md.: Johns Hopkins Press, 1961.

Lynd, Staughton. *Intellectual Origins of American Radicalism*. New York: Pantheon Books, 1968.

Lynn, Kenneth S. "The Regressive Historians." *American Scholar* 47, no. 4 (Autumn 1978): 471–500.

Mace, George. *Locke, Hobbes, and the Federalist Papers: An Essay on the Genesis of the American Political Heritage.* Carbondale: Southern Illinois University Press, 1979.

McColley, Robert. *Slavery and Jeffersonian Virginia.* Urbana: University of Illinois Press, 1973.

McCoy, Drew R. *The Elusive Republic: Political Economy in Jeffersonian America.* Chapel Hill: Published for the Institute for Early American History and Culture, Williamsburg, Virginia, by the University of North Carolina Press, 1980.

McDonald, Forrest. *Alexander Hamilton: A Biography.* New York: W. W. Norton & Co., 1979.

———. *The Presidency of Thomas Jefferson.* Lawrence: University Press of Kansas, 1976.

———. *We the People: The Economic Origins of the Constitution.* Chicago: University of Chicago Press, 1958.

Macpherson, C. B. *Democratic Theory: Essays in Retrieval.* Oxford: Clarendon Press, 1973.

———. *The Life and Times of Liberal Democracy.* Oxford: Oxford University Press, 1977.

———. *Political Theory of Possessive Individualism: Hobbes to Locke.* Oxford: Clarendon Press, 1962.

McWilliams, Wilson Carey. *The Idea of Fraternity in America.* Berkeley: University of California Press, 1973.

Madison, James. *The Mind of the Founder: Sources of the Political Thought of James Madison.* Edited by Marvin Meyers. Indianapolis and New York: Bobbs-Merrill Co., Inc., 1973.

———. *The Papers of James Madison.* Edited by William T. Hutchinson et al. 10 vols. Chicago: University of Chicago Press, 1962–77.

Malone, Dumas. "Introduction" to *Thomas Jefferson: The Man, His World, His Influence,* edited by Lally Weymouth. New York: G. P. Putnam's Sons, 1973.

———. *Jefferson and His Time.* 6 vols. Boston: Little, Brown & Company, 1948–81.

Mansfield, Harvey C., Jr. "Thomas Jefferson." In *American Political Thought: The Philosophic Dimension of American Statesmanship,* edited by Morton J. Frisch and Richard G. Stevens, pp. 23–50. New York: Charles Scribner's Sons, 1971.

Marcuse, Herbert. *Negations: Essays in Critical Theory.* Boston: Beacon Press, 1968.

Marx, Leo. *The Machine in the Garden: Technology and the Pastoral Ideal in America.* New York: Oxford University Press, 1964.

May, Henry F. *The End of American Innocence: A Study of the First Years of Our Own Time, 1912–1917.* Oxford and New York: Oxford University Press, 1979.

————. *The Enlightenment in America.* New York: Oxford University Press, 1976.

Meyer, Donald H. *The Democratic Enlightenment.* New York: G. P. Putnam's Sons, 1976.

Mill, John Stuart. "Considerations on Representative Government." In *"Utilitarianism," "On Liberty," and "Considerations on Representative Government,"* edited by H. B. Acton, chap. 8. London: J. M. Dent & Sons Ltd., 1972.

Miller, John Chester. *The Wolf by the Ears: Thomas Jefferson and Slavery.* New York: Free Press, 1977.

Morgan, Edmund Sears. *The Challenge of the American Revolution.* New York: W. W. Norton, 1976.

————. *Virginians at Home: Family Life in the Eighteenth Century.* Williamsburg, Va.: Colonial Williamsburg, Inc., 1952.

Murrin, John M. "The Great Inversion, or Court Versus Country: A Comparison of the Revolution Settlements in England (1688–1721) and America (1776–1816)." In *Three British Revolutions: 1641, 1688, 1776,"* edited by J. G. A. Pocock, pp. 368–453. Princeton, N.J.: Princeton University Press, 1980.

Paine, Thomas. *The Life and Works of Thomas Paine.* Edited by William M. van der Weyde. 10 vols. Patriots' ed. New Rochelle, N.Y.: Thomas Paine National Historical Association, 1925.

Parrington, Vernon Louis. *Main Currents in American Thought: An Interpretation of American Literature from the Beginning to 1920.* 3 vols. New York: Harcourt, Brace & Co., Inc., 1927–30.

Peterson, Merrill D. *The Jefferson Image in the American Mind.* New York: Oxford University Press, 1960.

————. *Thomas Jefferson: A Profile.* New York: Hill & Wang, 1967.

————. *Thomas Jefferson and the New Nation: A Biography.* New York: Oxford University Press, 1970.

Pocock, J. G. A. *The Ancient Constitution and the Feudal Law: A Study of English Historical Thought in the Seventeenth Century.* Cambridge: Cambridge University Press, 1957.

————. *The Machiavellian Moment: Florentine Political Thought and the Atlantic Republican Tradition.* Princeton, N.J.: Princeton University Press, 1975.

————. *Politics, Language and Time: Essays on Political Thought and History.* New York: Atheneum, 1971.

————, ed. *Three British Revolutions: 1641, 1688, 1776.* Princeton, N.J.: Princeton University Press, 1980.

Randall, John Hermann, Jr. *The Making of the Modern Mind.* 50th anniversary ed. New York: Columbia University Press, 1976.

Randolph, Sarah N., comp. *The Domestic Life of Thomas Jefferson.* New York: Frederick Ungar Publishing Co., 1958.

Rist, John M. *Epicurus: An Introduction.* Cambridge: Cambridge University Press, 1972.

————. *Stoic Philosophy*. London: Cambridge University Press, 1969.

Robinson, William A. *Jeffersonian Democracy in New England*. New Haven: Yale University Press, 1916.

Roelofs, H. Mark. *Ideology and Myth in American Politics: A Critique of a National Political Mind*. Boston and Toronto: Little, Brown & Co., 1976.

Rossiter, Clinton, ed. *Alexander Hamilton and the Constitution*. New York: Harcourt, Brace & World, 1964.

Rousseau, Jean-Jacques. *The First and Second Discourses*. Edited by Roger Masters and translated by Roger D. and Judith R. Masters. New York: St. Martin's Press, 1964.

————. *The Social Contract: Or, Principles of Political Right*. Edited by Charles M. Sherover. Rev. trans. New York: New Amerian Library, 1974.

Schachner, Nathan. *Thomas Jefferson: A Biography*. 2 vols. New York: Appleton-Century-Crofts, Inc., 1951.

Schlesinger, Arthur M. "The Lost Meaning of 'The Pursuit of Happiness.'" *William and Mary Quarterly* 21, no. 3 (July 1964): 325-27.

Scott, William B. *In Pursuit of Happiness: American Conceptions of Property from the Seventeenth to the Twentieth Century*. Bloomington: Indiana University Press, 1977.

Shalhope, Robert E. "Republicanism and Early American Historiography." *William and Mary Quarterly* 39, no. 2 (Apr. 1982): 334-56.

————. "Toward a Republican Synthesis: The Emergence of an Understanding of Republicanism in American Historiography." *William and Mary Quarterly* 29, no. 1 (Jan. 1972): 49-80.

Sheehan, Bernard W. *Seeds of Extinction: Jeffersonian Philanthropy and the American Indian*. New York: Published for the Institute of Early American History and Culture at Williamsburg, Virginia, by W. W. Norton, 1973.

Shklar, Judith. "Inventing America: Jefferson's Declaration of Independence by Garry Wills." *New Republic*. 26 Aug. and 2 Sept. 1978, pp. 32-34.

Skidmore, Max J. *American Political Thought*. New York: St. Martin's Press, 1978.

Smith, Henry Nash. *Virgin Land: The American West as Symbol and Myth*. Cambridge: Harvard University Press, 1950.

Spurlin, Paul Merrill. *Rousseau in America: 1760-1809*. University: University of Alabama Press, 1969.

Stourzh, Gerald. *Alexander Hamilton and the Idea of Republican Government*. Stanford, Calif.: Stanford University Press, 1970.

Strout, Cushing. "Liberalism, Conservatism and the Babel of Tongues." *Partisan Review* 25, no. 1 (Winter 1958): 101-9.

Takaki, Ronald T. *Iron Cages: Race and Culture in Nineteenth-Century America*. New York: Alfred A. Knopf, 1979.

Tocqueville, Alexis de. *Democracy in America*. 2 vols. New York: Schocken Books, 1961.

Tully, James. *A Discourse on Property: John Locke and His Adversaries*. Cambridge: Cambridge University Press, 1980.

Turner, Frederick Jackson. *The Significance of the Frontier in American History*. New York: H. Holt & Co., 1920.
Weber, Max. *The Protestant Ethic and the Spirit of Capitalism*. Translated by Talcott Parsons. New York: Oxford University Press, 1958.
White, Morton. *The Philosophy of the American Revolution*. New York: Oxford University Press, 1978.
———. *Pragmatism and the American Mind: Essays and Reviews in Philosophy and Intellectual History*. New York: Oxford University Press, 1973.
Williamson, Chilton. *American Suffrage: From Property to Democracy, 1760–1860*. Princeton, N.J.: Princeton University Press, 1960.
Wills, Garry. *Explaining America: The Federalist*. Garden City, N.Y.: Doubleday & Co., Inc., 1981.
———. *Inventing America: Jefferson's Declaration of Independence*. Garden City, N.Y.: Doubleday & Co., Inc., 1978.
Wilstach, Paul. *Jefferson and Monticello*. Garden City, N.Y.: Doubleday, Page & Co., 1925.
Wiltse, Charles Maurice. *The Jeffersonian Tradition in American Democracy*. Chapel Hill: University of North Carolina Press, 1935.
Wolin, Sheldon S. *Politics and Visions: Continuity and Innovation in Western Political Thought*. Boston: Little, Brown & Co., 1960.
Wood, Gordon S. *The Creation of the American Republic, 1776–1787*. Chapel Hill: Published for the Institute of Early American History and Culture at Williamsburg, Virginia, by the University of North Carolina Press, 1969.
Young, Alfred F., ed. *The American Revolution: Explorations in the History of American Radicalism*. Dekalb: Northern Illinois University Press, 1976.

Index

167

Printed in the United States
153425LV00002B/2/P

9 780700 602933